A JOURNEY BEYOND THE HORIZON

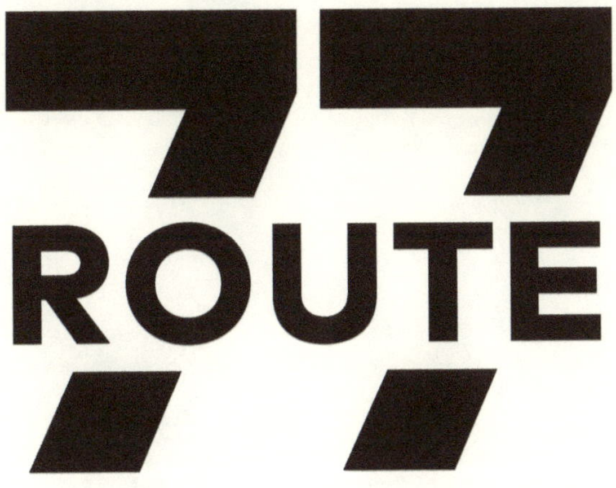

MAURITS TOMPOT

Paperback: 978-1-965632-35-2
eBook: 978-1-965632-36-9
Library of Congress Control Number: 2024921002

Ordering Information:

Prime Seven Media
518 Landmann St.
Tomah City, WI 54660

Printed in the United States of America

Table of Contents

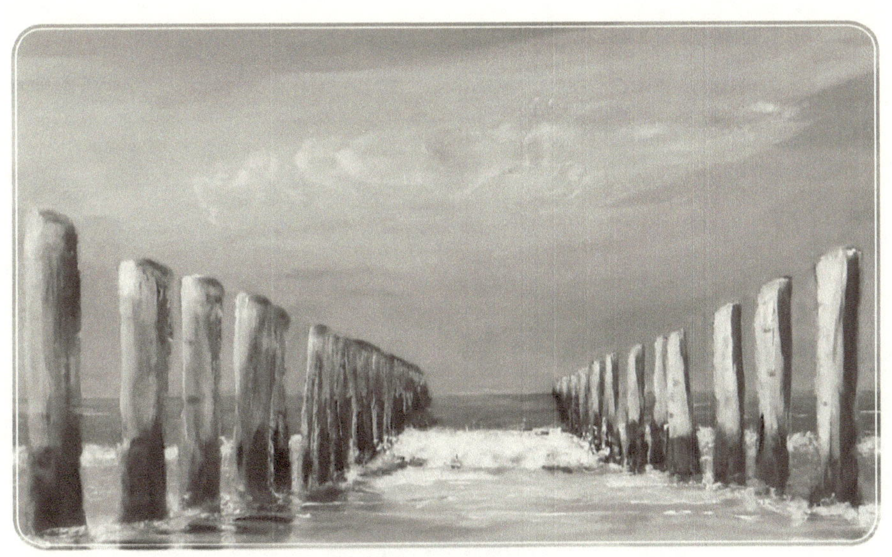

Foreword

I met Maurits_Tompot a few years ago when he was home-sitting for me in Cape Town, South Africa. He gave me his book in Dutch and although I speak Afrikaans, it was too difficult to read. When Maurits was back home in Holland, he started translating the book into English which I corrected as far as possible. Here is the result, his autobiography, a book of family life in Jakarta, excitement, intrigue, tragedy and ultimate submission with several 'stages or tokens', like Israel raised twelve stones as a monument after passing through the Jordan River. What a blessing to recall what God has done in our lives.

This is only half the story; the sequel, Route 777, is under construction.

Maurits thinks he is like Moses at the beginning of his ministry. 'Shakespeare is Here' will soon be published and a book about the pyramids of Giza is a new project.

What makes this book special is that Maurits is also an artist. He placed several paintings in the book to illustrate his story. While reading, please click on the QR Codes to see the pictures in colour and the explanation on his website www.mauritstompot.com

Charlotte Groenemeyer
Plumstead 27th October 2024

STAGE I

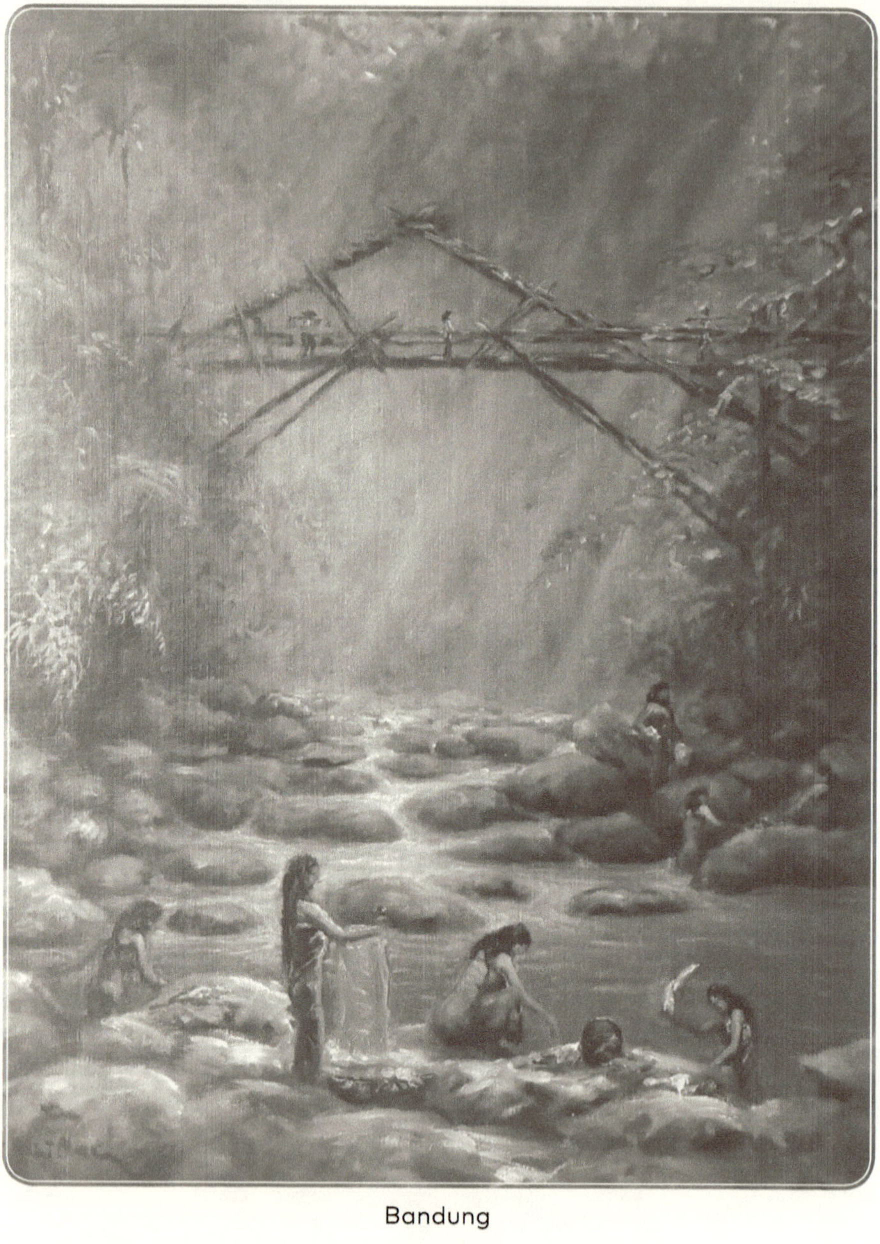

Bandung

Indonesia 1952

On March 9, 1952, I was born in Djakarta. The name on my birth announcement was Michiel and just as the name Batavia changed after independence to Djakarta or Jakarta, I was later called Maurits Rolff. It seemed that the director of the timber trade in Holland, whom my father worked for, was called Maurits.

In Kebajoran, Block O II, we lived in a spacious bungalow and colonial life was tempo doeloe—good. In addition to the many holidays in Bandung, Mother organized numerous tea parties and feasts until early morning. Ballantine whisky arrived in wooden crates, which Jon, my brother and I used to store our dinky toys.

One day, baboe Attemie brought me into the room with the rattan chairs and the maid cleared her throat loudly, saying, 'Here I am, Madam!'

Startled Mother looked up with furrowed brows from behind her pedal sewing machine and saw the servant wide-eyed. With her index finger in front of her mouth, she pointed to the bottom of the curtain with the other hand, two men's brown feet protruded. Mother saw it and without hesitation grabbed a pair of scissors from one of the unfolded blades and yanked the curtain aside. The burglar was shocked and fled. Mother pulled me towards herself and lifted me. Sobbing with fright, I asked why the Javanese man was hiding there. Trembling, she shook her head and sighed, 'It's okay, Mauki, he will never return!'

I didn't understand; our garden boys often hid among the pisang or banana trees.

A few months later, Tuan Tompot was threatened by his chauffeur on the driveway to the garage. At gunpoint, Father was forced to hand over the keys to his jeep.

Since Sukarno, the President of the new Republic, wanted to liberate Indonesia from foreigners, intimidation and burglaries were increasing and after Father's long urging, Mother and her three children embarked on the 'Willem Ruys' end in 1958. I was six, Jonneke eight and sister Jolanthe four. Black-and-white photographs show Father waving at us, standing in his white shirt and shorts on the quay of Tanjong Priok. Mother used her white handkerchief to dab her tear-filled eyes. Would they see each other again? Jonneke was waving with his white plaster cast on his arm. I can still hear that crack when he broke his wrist falling off the swing a few weeks before leaving. At the sight of Mother's tears, I asked why Daddy was not going with us to Holland. 'He still has business to settle and will come by aeroplane as soon as possible.'

After the big ropes were thrown loose, a tugboat towed the ship while the horn blared so loudly that my body trembled. Later in colour films, with the rattling sound, we saw images of sun-drenched Singapore, flying fish on the ocean, Port Saïd, and the Suez Canal. As tropical children, we always walked barefoot, and when passing Gibraltar, we had to wear shoes that pinched our feet. The woollen clothes, smelling of camphor, itched terribly.

STAGE 2

Holland

In the middle of winter, the Tompot family arrived in Holland. Steam clouds escaped my mouth and an icy white powder tinged my hands. The house at Midden Geestweg No. 7 in Bergen, North Holland, had now been rented for six months. The smell of coal from the smoking chimneys and the chirp of seagulls still reminds me of that period.

At the white-painted Van Reenen School, a tall Dutch teacher, Ms. Schermerhorn, deeply impressed me. Everything in Holland was thorough and by appointment. I wanted to become a veterinarian, as I liked to play on the farm of my friend Maarten. Days later, my clothes would still smell sour from cows and hay.

At the end of Midden Geestweg, we could enter the large forest. Gnomes were supposed to sit on red-and-white toadstools, but as an imaginative boy, I stayed within the limits of decency.

In the evening, all the children from the neighbourhood would gather on the street to play. Even the lovely daughters of the art painter Karel Colnot, who lived next door in that mysterious house hidden between the huge trees, joined us. On Wednesday afternoons, we experienced the magic of watching television at a neighbour's house. Ultimately, as the image disappeared from the screen into a white dot that slowly disappeared, it remained magically spectacular.

After returning from Indonesia, Father was allowed to choose from various surrounding countries to set up a new timber trade for the Utrecht company. For the next seven years, we would stay in Vilvoorde in Flanders, Belgium.

STAGE 3

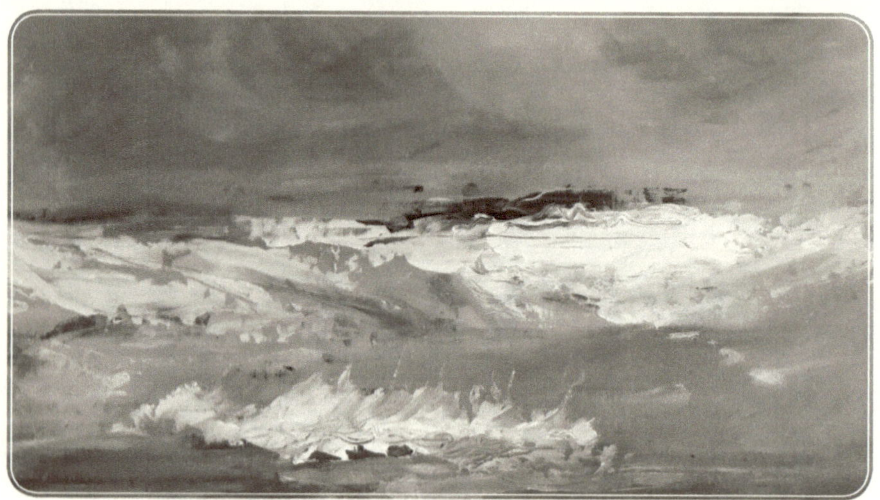

The sea doesn't teach you how to swim.

Belgium

In Vilvoorde was no forest or beach. We lived in the narrow Frans Geldersstraat at No. 27, above the office of Treetex Acoustics. Behind our house, a large coal factory spewed out its smelly steam every ten minutes. Our new playground extended from the dark basement to the high-walled, restricted space of the courtyard. Here, children never played on the streets, and I became homesick, missing the beauty of Bergen. It made my belly ache.

Father was busy setting up a new business with only one typist/secretary and four representatives arriving every Saturday morning. Together with Dad, they smoked until his office was a blue haze.

I remember how Father took me to the new school, wearing his brown raincoat. In a room with barely any daylight, thirty Flemish-speaking children watched me. After Daddy left, I felt displaced and cried, but at the same time, I was ashamed. The teacher asked what was wrong, and I made up a story that my sandal was pinching. He knelt and unfastened my footwear, but the tears kept flowing. This gentleman in the first class and the one in the sixth were the only normal teachers in my opinion. The other masters had strange characteristics, like the 'Bolle' from the fourth grade. He had been in the army for a long time, and he only let us march in the gym—left, right, left, right. He punished us by making us kneel on a square cookie tin at the front of the class. Balancing on your kneecaps was the least painful; otherwise, the sharp edges of the box would cut into your shins. I managed to bribe the Bolle with boxes of cigars, 'smuggled' out of Father's client gift drawer.

Mr. Donville from the fifth grade, had a hunchback and we called him 'Don Quixote.' Almost every day, at the back of the classroom, he gave me a lukewarm slice of his mandarin. Yet he would hit my fingers with a steel ruler if I misbehaved.

My brother Jon and I were the only Protestant children to receive special religious education. To this end, a certain Mr. De Lange travelled weekly by tram 58 from Brussels to teach us separately from each other. Simeon, the red-haired Jewish boy, was taught by a rabbi, and for the rest of the class, a priest would come in wearing a black cassock with a white collar.

Bible stories fascinated me very much, and as a private pupil, I was always allowed to ask questions. 'Sir, how did all the animals fit into Noah's Ark?'

'Well, Mauki, only one pair of butterflies, one pair of ducks or dogs were allowed. Not all species and I think the Lord sent little giraffes, elephants, and hippos to the ark.'

I kept mice in the basement and asked how Noah, his three sons and their wives could feed all the animals and clean the pens. Mr. De Lange suggested a simple year of hibernation.

After the exciting adventures of David, his son Solomon was featured. 'Sir, how could the wise King Solomon become unwise?'

'Wisdom is a person, Mauki. If you stray from Him, you also lose wisdom. Do you understand?' Yes, I did, because once on Vlieland, I drifted away from Father while swimming in the sea, but he could pull me out of the strong current just in time.

Many Bible stories are difficult to understand, such as Abraham's sacrifice. How could God ask a father to do such a thing?

'You have to wait until the Easter holidays to hear the answer. Now, let's look at my stamps. I have an almost complete stamp collection from Israel and several African countries with wild animals.' Carefully, using tweezers, treasures emerged from behind transparent paper sheets.

On Sunday, Mother drove us to the Protestant Church in Brussels, where she hoped to meet other Dutch expats. I found the Sunday school classroom cold and dull. Father always stayed at home, peeling potatoes while the radio spewed out football results that sounded like formulas to me—Ajax, Feyenoord or Heracles.

Sunday afternoons, however, were the highlight of the week, when the family would walk in the surrounding nature reserves like Hofstade, Grimbergen, or Tervuren. Father taught us how to birdwatch, and he later bought a holiday bungalow near a bird sanctuary. Yet, the seagulls there screeched less exuberantly than in Bergen or on Vlieland, where we spent our summer holidays in a bungalow called 'Jolly Day'. The journey to the Wadden Islands felt like a world trip and we spent the night in the windy village of Huisduinen, where most fences were crooked. We slept on rubber air mattresses, and the next morning we drove over the endless Afsluitdijk to distant Friesland. In Harlingen, we felt being abroad, surrounded by Frisians and Germans. The rocking boat, surrounded by a cloud of seagulls, carried us to 'the edge of the world.'

When Father's timber trade flourished, a villa with a spacious courtyard was rented on the Elewijtse Steenweg in Eppegem. Further along the cobblestone road, towards the Rubens Castle, a piece of land was later purchased for a model house to showcase the various types of wood used in his business. After moving to

Eppegem, we tough Dutch boys had to cycle to school in Vilvoorde through all sorts of weather.

In the first year of secondary school, Latin and later Greek were taught and I liked learning. As the best student in the class, you entered an exciting competition with official award ceremonies during such occasions, laureates wore smart jackets, white shirts, and ties.

In Eppegem, I felt almost as happy as I did in Bergen. My potatoes, radishes, carrots, and strawberries thrived in a section of the huge garden. I had rabbits grazing in a homemade, movable, spacious run, which kept the lawn tidy. The village butcher gave me money for mature animals, though it made me nauseous because of their big, frightened eyes when I handed them over. My sadness disappeared while romping in the meadows around the Rubens Castle. I secretly smoked my first wooden pipe at the end of the Steenweg and Christiane lived there. She already looked more than grown-up at the age of sixteen and was even ready for a new set of teeth, like her brother or parents had gotten at an early age. I often told her brother Ed not to give his rabbit cow parsley. After hardly eating it, they would lose weight and die.

One day after school, we arrived at Christiane's house and saw the outside door wide open. Inside, all the cupboards were opened and the contents were scattered all over the floor. Fearing burglars still upstairs, I wanted to flee but Christiane bravely picked up the phone and called the police and her parents. Since that time, I have always warned people to be careful with their belongings.

My curiosity about the female sex was growing, maybe because boys and girls were separated in Belgian schools. That summer in Vlieland, I built huts in the dunes with a bright blonde German girl named Heidi.

During the foundation laying for the model home, unexpectedly, baby Ruud was born. Life smiled on spending the beautiful Pentecost weekend of 1966 with the family of Koos, Father's eldest brother, who lived in Huisduinen. I proudly showed off my young crow, 'Sesam', which I had taken from an 'abandoned' nest along with another one for my friend Jos Bolsens, My father doubted the truth and asked me, 'How do you know that the nest was abandoned, Mauki?'

'We didn't see the parents anywhere.'

Father shook his head with a grim grin and with the arrival of these black birds, ominous clouds gathered on the horizon for the Tompot and the Bolsens families.

The Pentecost weekend was sunny and perfect for lawn games and badminton. We made cousin Rob laugh again while peeling a mountain of peanuts at the kitchen table. Rob screeched so infectiously that everyone kept laughing. I would spend many holidays in Switzerland with him before everything changed.

The night after the family left, Father felt pressure on his chest. The doctor from Zemst arrived and diagnosed it as the flu. He advised a week of rest but Father asked, 'Is it not my heart, doctor?' After all, some grandparents had died of heart failure. Father led a sedentary existence, smoking two packets of unfiltered Lexington's a day.

After a week's rest, Father left for the office on Monday morning, and the first thing he planned to do was sign the life insurance papers for the new house. That simple signature would determine the future of my mother and her four children.

In the course of that bright spring day, a black car arrived in front of the white fence before the driveway. A man in a black suit stepped out onto the gravel path. Little Rudy stood in front of the window with his toes in the nylon net of the playpen. Suddenly, my mother grabbed my hand and pulled me toward the front door. She trembled as the man spoke, and soon she began to weep. Something bad must have happened and I wanted to flee and run up the stairs, but Mother held me until the vicar came inside.

Later, it turned out that Father had died of a heart attack and we children never saw him again, nor did we attend the funeral in Huisduinen. I kept hoping Dad was in Sweden on business, but the green Opel Rekord never drove into the yard again. The father of my friend Jos also died that same year, and Sesam, the crow, got lost during the holiday in Vlieland.

Three months later, our neighbour Uncle Hein also developed chest pressure at night, and the village doctor made the same diagnosis. After he left, Hein's wife, Maria, knocked on our door in a panic. Mother immediately called an ambulance and Uncle Hein barely survived. He was still given time to sign the life insurance papers. Three years later, he died, and 'Aunt' Maria was able to continue living in her beautiful bungalow

STAGE 4

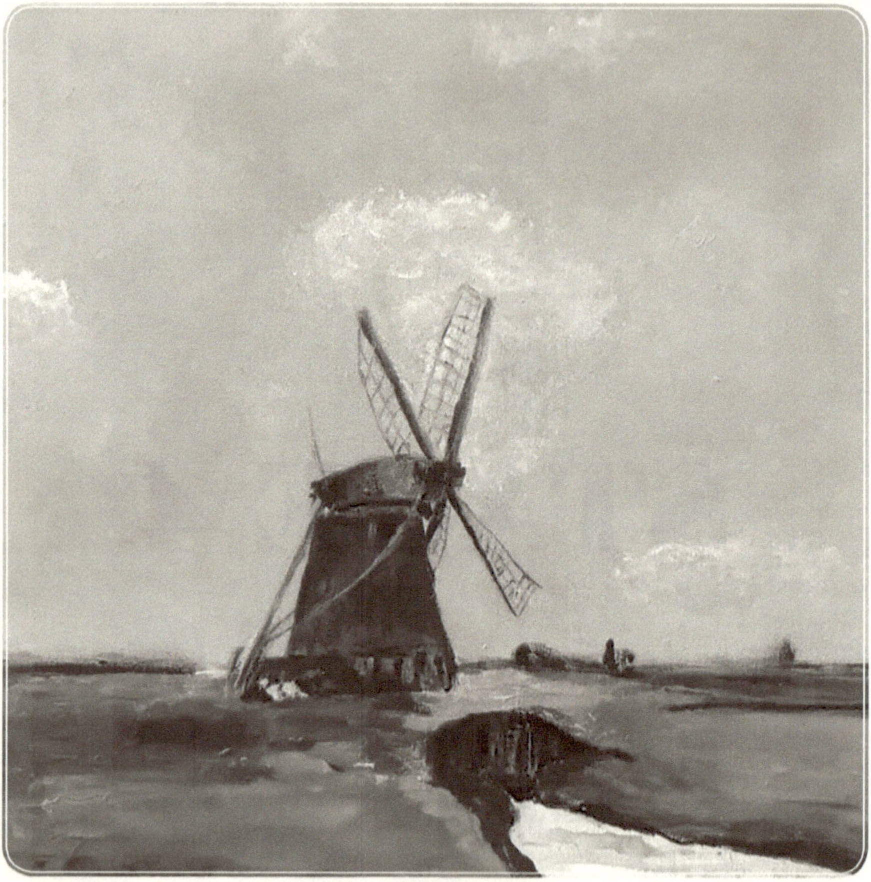

Copy of J.H. Weissenbruch

The Netherlands

Mother's widow's pension was not abundant and thanks to contacts in Brussels, she applied for a job at the State Lottery in the Netherlands. Selling lottery tickets from home would be ideal with her growing offspring.

Mrs. Tompot was successful in her application for the State Lottery Sales position. She could even choose from three vacancies and Gouda was the most convenient location between the family in North Holland and her Belgian friends. The building plot in Eppegem and the summer house in Zeeuws Vlaanderen were sold and an upper-class house on the Martenssingel in Gouda was bought. Compared to the villa in Eppegem, we children found the house with the small garden rather boring.

Jon left to complete a school year at the Lyceum in Gouda. He became a boarder on the Kattensingel, and at thirteen years old, I was now seen as the eldest son.

I had to settle in like an exotic bird at the Coornhert Gymnasium. Ballroom dancing with girls to the music of a Dixieland band was a complete culture shock. Like a wallflower, I looked around until a girl with a sturdy body invited me to dance.

'No, no, I really can't!'

'It doesn't matter, come, I'll teach you the quickstep.'

Hanneke pulled me onto the dance floor, where I had to learn three steps, quickly. The sensation of this full-figured young lady pressing against my body was exciting. From that evening on, we would often visit each other until my mother, who had been in the resistance during the war with my father in Den Helder, heard Hanneke's last name. It was connected with the NSB and the Nazis and my friendship with Hanneke was no longer tolerated.

Marja was the prettiest girl in the class and she arrived at the next school party in an open sports car. Her older brother brought and fetched her again. She looked glamorous, wearing a leather jacket. Even years later, when we met in Renesse, her eyes, the smell of her breath or the sound of her voice did not create the right chemistry.

Mother was doing extremely well in business and within a few years, the whole family could travel by train for winter sports in Kitzbühel. A year later, we even flew to Filzmoos. The picturesque Austria or the Mediterranean ambience of Spanish Altea made a deep impression on me. During camping holidays in Switzerland with cousin Rob's family, the sublime beauty of nature constantly impressed me.

Mother's business success was due to a simple formula that today is called customer loyalty. She noted topics from the last conversation on used envelopes with the tickets ordered, such as illness, death, birth, marriage, or divorce. Moreover, she spent a lot of time with her clients, leaving little or no attention to me or so it felt to me. When I got home from school, I had to make tea and serve it to her behind the counter in the front room. The most important woman in my young adolescent life was missing and soon, I began to seek out my friends' mothers, where warm attention was present at tea time. This search for that important figure may have shaped my behaviour toward women.

During school holidays, Mother took us to summer camps in the hope of some re-education. As a teenager, Ruud was even enrolled in a Belgian sports boarding school, where authority still prevailed. As a thirteen-year-old, he was already travelling alone by train on weekends.

I remember the visit of two elders from the Dutch Reformed Church. Both wore black jackets and trousers with white pinstripes. Next to the front door, they had probably seen the State Lottery emblem of the orange fish. At the end of the visit, after the prayer, they admonished Mother to stop playing the lottery because it is gambling. They demanded that she resign.

'Yes, but how am I expected to feed my children?'

Both men were unanimous in their statement that the Lord would provide. Mrs. Tompot would leave this church forever.

Father's death had shaken me like a mental concussion, and I started searching for the meaning of life. I was far too young to delve into philosophy, from Socrates to Sartre. I attended yoga classes and learned Buddhist meditation techniques from an artist in Bodegraven. I began to admire this "enlightened" guru, but I noticed that his Swiss wife was a Christian who refused to accept this cult.

The father of my girlfriend Yvonne gave me a voluminous book titled, 'The Great Pyramid, Its Divine Massage'. I was impressed by the detailed description of the Pyramid of Giza, one of the seven wonders of the world. The missing top stone would be a finger pointing to the 'Cornerstone', rejected by humanity. In the King's Chamber, a huge tomb was empty, symbolising the Resurrection of the King. The dimensions of the corridors were said to depict prophetic timetables for His return. The many calculations were beyond my comprehension, but they seemed to provide evidence of a Higher Intelligence, as incontrovertible as the Great Pyramid itself. The book hit me like a 'stone'.

In third grade, I became rebellious and wore red, yellow, and purple corduroy trousers, while the school dress code was blue or grey. At the end of the school year, I had to retake a Greek exam and spent the hot summer of 1968 crammed in a room upstairs at my godparents' house in the super boring city of Zwijndrecht. Finally, I memorized Xenophon's translation by heart, yet the teacher downgraded me and I had to leave this elite grammar school.

Mother was using her charm to persuade the headmaster of the Christian Lyceum to admit me and she succeeded. I was admitted to the fourth grade, although I was one year ahead in Greek and one year behind in German.

My fresh start was cancelled due to Pfeiffer's disease, which caused the cervical glands in my throat to swell. Thanks to penicillin, I could breathe again, but the chronic fatigue lingered and my motivation to succeed at school vanished completely.

By Christmas, I had recovered enough and started to deliver newspapers very early in the morning. There was a lot of money to collect with New Year's tips. During the daytime, I fixed mopeds and often rode noisy, smoking bikes over the Martenssingel to the Karnemelksloot and back again.

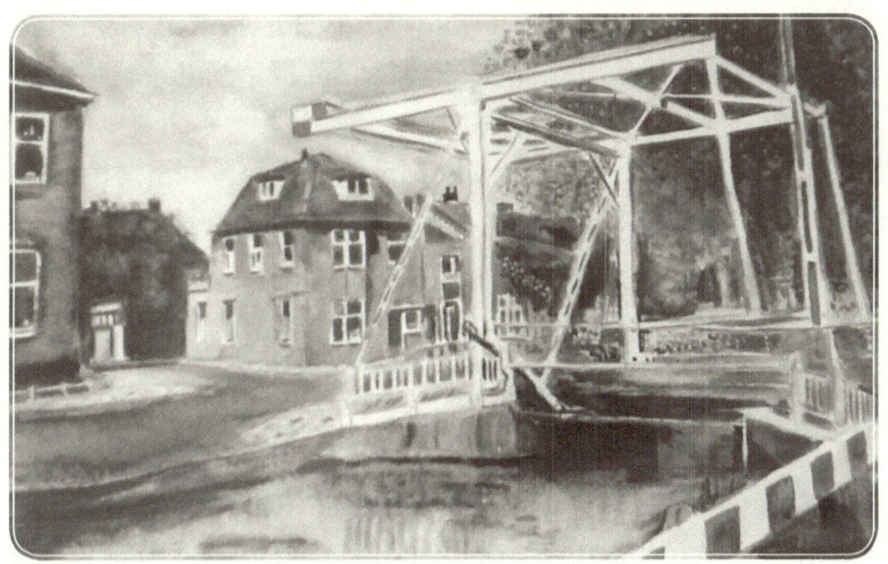

Watercolour on paper Karnemelksloot

At the weekends, I visited performances by soul bands in the surrounding villages and with my red five-gear Garelli, I easily passed my friends on their black Puchs or Tomos, all equipped with high handlebars and round rear lights. Later, I tinkered with antique motorcycles such as the Hercules, Panther, and the Indian Scout—the absolute top. I fell in love with the matte red vehicle that emerged from under the straw-like scrap metal in a garage shed. I covered the bare saddle with new leather in the handwork class at school, and for a front light, I drove to Amsterdam; for a rear light, I made it to Rotterdam. I became a member of a unique international club of Indian Scout owners and cherished my bike as a treasure. How foolish can a man be to fall in love with a piece of rusty metal?

My hard-working mother grew annoyed with me and kicked me down the stairs, screaming, 'Get out of my house and don't come back unless you have a proper job!

As an eighteen-year-old, I was on the street, and where was I supposed to go? The library provided me with a dry and warm place where I could browse the newspapers for job advertisements. That same day, I managed to get a job as an apprentice photographer in Rotterdam. Triumphantly, I came home and told my mother about my future workplace.

The long days in the darkroom with the chemical odours began to oppress me, especially when the owner started visiting me in the evenings, coming too close. During the coffee breaks in the photo studio, I went through the newspaper ads again and found a travel agency looking for catering staff at a mansion in Austria. That same afternoon, I was invited to meet the director, and I showed up apologising for my faded denim suit. To my great surprise, I got the job within fifteen minutes.

STAGE 5

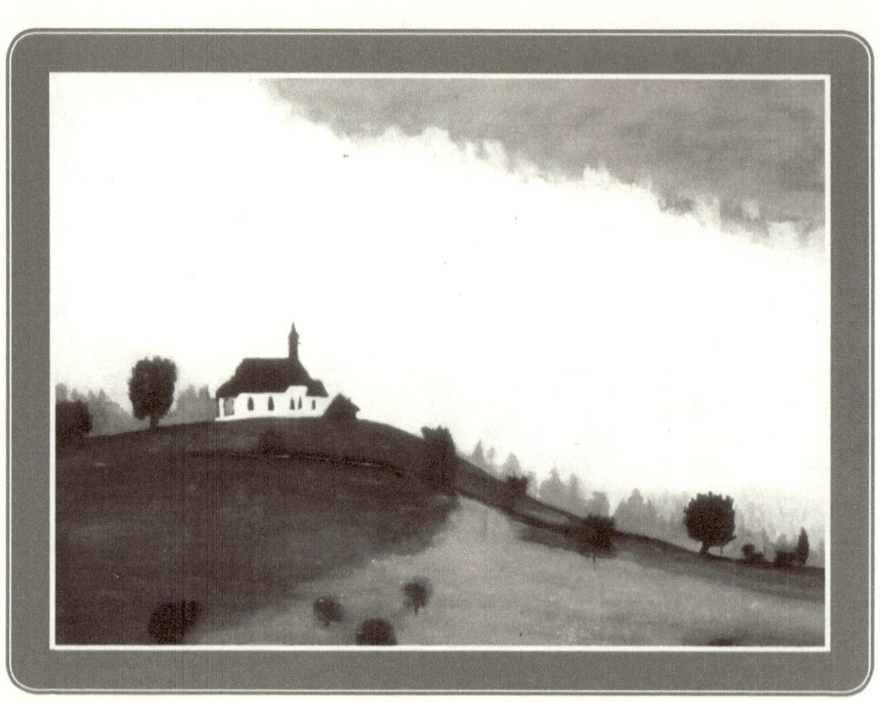

Austria

On April 30, 1970, I boarded an almost empty coach in Rotterdam with the Brand couple and a twenty-year-old chambermaid named Anja. The driver took us to the lovely manor Luisenheim, perfectly situated along the lake of Millstatt. The Brands had a Rotterdam accent and Anja had a Zeelandic-Flemish accent.

Mr. Brand was scrawny and constantly walked his little dog while smoking little cigars and his voluminous wife had the strange habit of lifting her heavy bosom with both hands.

To the right of the impressive stairs leading to the garden, I found a room full of garden furniture. Except for one chair and a table, I moved everything outside onto the terrace and set up my domicile inside. Every morning when I woke up, the lake sparkled and the birds gave an impressive concert. I sniffed the fresh air, and in the kitchen, I was welcomed by the smell of fresh Kaiserbrötchen, delivered by the Austrian baker, who spoke a strange German. Some villagers still dressed in lederhosen or dirndls with enchanting cleavages. Once, a woman came to apply for a job as a waitress in this dress, her cleavage glistening with sweat, and black hairs poking between her breasts. She didn't get the job.

Nevertheless, the happiness I had experienced in Bergen or Vlieland bubbled up again, I had found my destiny.

To drive out the winter cold from the large rooms, I chopped wood for the large tiled stoves and helped Anja make beds in the many rooms. The newly arrived tour guide was also called Anja and she asked me to assist her in exploring the many taverns around Millstätter See. Although she was ten years older, we soon dreamed of renting the lovely empty castle at the bottom of the lake for the next tourist season.

When the first hotel guests arrived, I operated as a bellboy, then donned a white jacket to be a waiter at dinner and a bartender in the evenings. The next morning, I helped serve breakfast and worked as a gardener. Thanks to Father's Rolleiflex camera, I had a professional appearance, photographing the hotel guests during the afternoons or evenings. In my free time, I rested on a desolate jetty on the other side of the lake, basking in the sun. A blonde Austrian girl, Gaby, also appeared there. She had the most beautiful blue eyes, surrounded by dark eyelashes and eyebrows. She didn't know how ferociously attractive she was in her self-crocheted bikini. As a future teacher, she did holiday work as a waitress in the imposing Schlossvilla mansion.

On my free evenings, Anja and I invited hotel guests for a tour along the 'Kneipen' or cosy wooden bars. The lights of the grand and mundane taverns along the lake twinkled on the terraces. The view was fabulous, like something from a fairy tale and so was my life.

As in fairy tales, witches appear to stop all happiness. Mother settled down for the summer holidays at a campsite in Döbriach, at the end of Millstätter See. Under her wings, a large family followed. I didn't know about the secret contact she had with the management of the travel agency I worked for, to terminate my employment. To ensure it, my brother Jon had to find a summer job close to me so I would surely return at the end of the season. He indeed found an opportunity to become a driver for a VW van at the same hotel where Gaby worked as a waitress. He knew German far better than I did and a strong competitor had arrived. She would have to choose between two brothers.

As we sat drinking coffee at the campsite, my mother suddenly dropped the announcement, 'Maurits, you have to return home in three weeks.'

Surprised, I asked, 'What? Who decided this?'

'You should go back to school,' she replied.

'No, I have a contract with the company in Rotterdam.'

'It's already been arranged with the agency and also with Mr. Brand', she said.

'Arranged with Rotterdam and the Brands'? Behind my back?'

I could barely believe this.

'It's better to have a degree, trust me' she insisted.

I felt betrayed and anger bubbled inside me. I wanted to swear loudly, but I held back for other tourists. I stood up, storming and leaving the campsite, cursing. As I walked away, I could faintly hear my mother saying, 'Oh, he'll get over it.'

I wouldn't get over it. I was devastated. Not only my plan to travel with the hotel staff to Kitzbühel for the winter season was crumbled, but also my connection with Gaby and the future I had envisioned with Anja for the next summer season was shattered. I enjoyed the tourist industry and the irony was that years later, I would indeed find myself working in a similar sector after taking many detours.

Back at Luisenheim, I searched for my passport, planning to escape. Soon I discovered that Mother had already given it to Mr. Brand for safekeeping and the bus driver would only return it upon my arrival in the Netherlands.

While I was seething, only Gaby could comfort me, 'In a few years, you will be free to see me in Austria!' she reassured me.

I said my goodbyes to both Anjas but avoided the Brands, who had been part of my mother's plot.

STAGE 6

Gouda

In a coach packed with departing hotel guests, I reluctantly returned to the Netherlands and soon enough, I found myself back in the confines of a school desk. Surrounded by much younger students, I felt suffocated, sinking into a swamp of inward rage. The frustration gnawed at me, leaving me isolated and angry. My mood became almost Hamlet-like in its melancholy.

Mother, concerned about my withdrawn and depressed state, took me to see a doctor. In a brief consultation, he barely scratched the surface of what I was going through and without much discussion, he prescribed Valium, which I began taking. The step from Valium to other drugs became dangerously small.

Around this time, I reconnected with an old schoolmate, John, who had also been expelled from the same elite grammar school. He was living as a squatter in Breda, adopting the hippie lifestyle. I didn't know that John had become a drug dealer and during the weekends, I would ride my motorcycle to visit him. We'd spend those days getting heavily stoned, sinking further into a haze that seemed to offer a fleeting escape from reality.

In Lyceum High School, I met Ton and Theo, two handsome guys my age who shared my love for literature. We found a way to indulge our interests while working as hosts in two cinemas in Gouda, taking turns on shifts so we could watch all the films for free. We were captivated by movies like *Woodstock* and *Easy Rider,* and I often found myself singing along to Steppenwolf's soundtrack,

'Born to be wild, get your motor running,

Head out on the highway, looking for adventure!'

Though I got along well with both of them, there was never any friendship between Ton and Theo. With Theo, I spent hours walking our dogs through the polders surrounding Gouda or sailing on his boat across the Reeuwijkse Lakes. During one summer holiday, we hitchhiked to France, where we fantasized about buying a farm and starting a campsite. Theo did buy a farm but without me.

With Ton, who would later become a journalist, I had deep discussions about newspaper articles, played endless games of chess and also hitchhiked along the *Route du Soleil*. On one particularly harrowing trip, our lives were endangered when we hitched a ride with a reckless driver. The man, who had already lost his lower limbs in a previous car accident, seemed to have learned nothing from it. He sped wildly down the infamous French three-lane roads, constantly overtaking other cars. I shouted over and over, "Slow down, sir, slowly please!'

Anton screamed along with me, but our cries went unheard. Finally, in desperation, I punched the crazed driver and shouted at him to stop immediately, 'Arrêtez! Stop au nom de Dieu!' He finally slowed down, and we leapt out of the car, trembling and grateful to be alive.

Years later, on a sunny Pentecost, I found myself hitchhiking again, this time to a conference in Vierhouten. The driver who picked me up boasted confidently about his driving skills from the very start, and soon we were recklessly speeding down the winding roads of the Veluwe. I demanded that he slow down, but instead of listening, he pressed harder on the gas. My worst fear became reality as the car lost control and flew out of the curve, heading straight for a concrete electricity building. I braced for impact, squeezing my eyes shut, and waiting for the inevitable crash. Miraculously, the car veered into a ditch just before colliding with the building and then bounced back onto the road. I scrambled out of the smoking vehicle, shaking, as the driver shouted with pride, 'Wasn't that excellent skill?' I was left speechless, standing in shock as he laughed and sped away, tyres screeching. That day, I made a vow: I would never hitchhike again. I took public transport home, thankful to have survived yet another close call.

In the meantime, my mother had grown increasingly frustrated with my antisocial behaviour. She arranged for me to stay with 'Aunt Alice,' an Indonesian acquaintance who also worked with her at the State Lottery. She lived on the sixth floor of an apartment building in one of the most depressing neighbourhoods in Gouda. Despite enjoying her delicious Indonesian food and how she cared for me, I skipped school constantly. By the time the final exams came around, I was too stoned to focus and unsurprisingly, failed but that same year, I managed to obtain my car, truck, and motorcycle licenses.

I was avenging my mother's betrayal, just like Shakespeare's Hamlet, because I still harboured resentment for how she had shattered my Austrian fairy tale. I felt an intense desire to leave the Netherlands and start a new life elsewhere as soon as possible.

Maybe I could make quick money by climbing the social ladder as a window cleaner. It seemed like an easy way to earn a lot, however, the reality of climbing up and down ladders for eight hours a day turned out to be physically exhausting for a twenty-year-old student. By the end of each weekend, I was barely able to recover. My boss, De Slegte - 'the Bad one', made the hard work more miserable for three gruelling months. He cursed at me when I dropped a sponge and from day one, he said I would never become a good window cleaner, but later I learned more about 'the Gouda Stained Windows'. Luckily, I was paired with a quirky coworker from a gypsy camp in Zwammerdam whose sense of humour helped me survive those draining months.

Where was the grass greenest? The kibbutz in Israel seemed like the best place to be. I envisioned an ideal society, where everything worked together in harmony. I planned to buy a cheap, 350cc two-stroke Jawa motorcycle, something I could easily discard if it broke down. Mother insisted on getting something safer and even offered to pay. Since she was covering the cost, I opted for a refurbished 250cc, one-cylinder BMW chopper, built in 1952— the year I was born. The money she gave me felt like bribery for the happiness she had stolen from me, but I accepted it anyway. I didn't tell her of a close brush with death I had experienced on Theo's bike. That incident occurred after a weekend at John's place in Breda. I had borrowed Theo's bike and was riding back home, heavily stoned, when disaster nearly struck. I was overtaking a truck with a trailer, speeding at 120 km per hour, when suddenly the rear tyre blew. The only thing that saved us from crashing was John's weight, which kept the bike from spinning out of control. Somehow, I managed to pull ahead of the truck and veer off onto the hard shoulder. Even after the repair at the garage, I was still shaking with fear.

Nerves shot, I asked John to take over the handlebars on the quiet polder roads near Moordrecht, even though he didn't have a driver's license. As I handed him the bike, he was standing on the soft verge and the weight of the Matchless dragged him hissing headfirst into the ditch. Slowly, John rose out of the duckweed, looking like a drenched Hare Krishna, with his round glasses resembling green Olympic circles alongside the two bike tyres. His hair and face were crowned with green algae, forming a tiara. The sight was so absurd that I couldn't stop laughing. The sheer ridiculousness of it finally calmed my frayed nerves but John wasn't amused at all. He stood there, dripping wet, stinking like a cesspit, utterly furious. After managing to pull out the bike, the engine rattled like an old lion and John shivered from the cold. He opted to sit on the back again, teeth chattering.

By the end of the summer, I felt ready for my world trip. My friend Ton, unexpectedly, expressed a desire to join me, eager to experience a great adventure of his own. This meant he would have to refuse military service, which was a significant decision. I had already been exempted after a school doctor showed me how to fail the hearing test.

Anduze

The day of our departure arrived and Ton showed up with a giant backpack. A military helmet and a waterproof army sleeping bag completed his luggage. We were sent off by family members with barely disguised amusement. My sister asked, 'How far is this journey, gentlemen?' We weren't taken seriously and as if to validate her scepticism, we barely made it across the border near Antwerp before we encountered our first setback. The engine began making loud bangs from afterburning.

Luckily, a friendly Flemish mechanic came to our rescue. With just a quarter turn of his screwdriver, he adjusted the faulty ignition—for free! We were back on the road but in France, the sky looked ominously dark and yet, strangely, there was a constant corridor of blue above us. It was as if Providence was watching over us, allowing us to ride without getting drenched. I took it as a great miracle, though Ton was not impressed.

Arriving in Paris, we visited the Sacré-Coeur, where a group of old and young people sang religious hymns on the steps. Ton, bemused, turned to me, asking, 'Are these foolish people part of some sect?'

I had no answer, but it struck me. Why were these ordinary young people, so much like us, praising God in public?

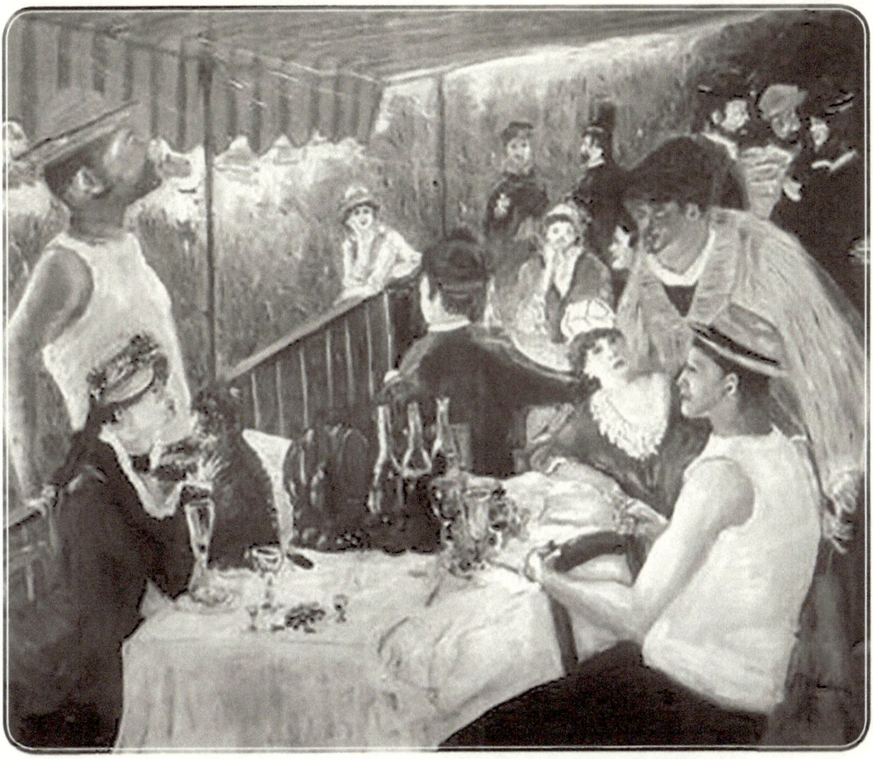

Copy Renoir

That night, we found a dimly lit park on the outskirts of Paris to roll out our army sleeping bags. After finishing a bottle of red wine, we settled down for what we hoped would be a peaceful night's sleep. What had seemed like a quiet park, turned out to be a thoroughfare for people heading to work in the morning. As we groggily made tea on a small butane gas stove and spread cheese on a baguette, the commuters gave us odd glances. From then on, we decided to avoid urban spots and camp in the countryside, where we made do with tea and soaked stale bread for breakfast. We pressed on down the Route du Soleil, eventually arriving in Anduze, in the South of France. There, we stayed in a 'château' owned by our popular religious teacher from the Christian Lyceum. Early in the morning, we worked in his vineyard, weeding the rows of vines until the heat became unbearable. Afternoons were spent swimming in a river that wound through apricots and peach orchards and the evenings were filled with philosophical discussions lasting late into the night. We drank copious amounts of wine—every other day I'd hop on the motorcycle and ride to the local cooperative, where I filled a 10-litre jerrycan with wine as though it were gas fuel.

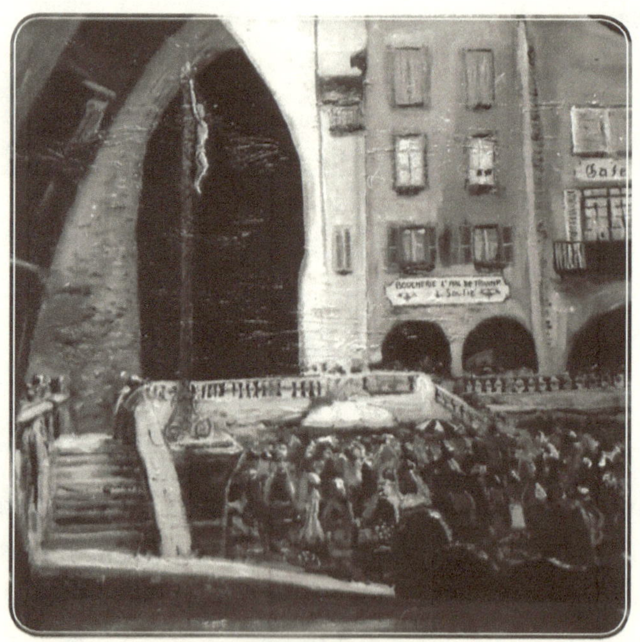

Vive la France

Our teacher/pastor often spoke about renowned figures like Martin Luther King, Nelson Mandela and Che Guevara, highlighting their courage and dedication to justice. In the quiet village of Anduze, we heard about another figure—the Man from Nazareth. Anduze was one of the few Protestant strongholds in the South of France, a little town where faith seemed more palpable than in the world of ideologies we had heard so much about. Precisely that week, a group of young people had arrived to carry out an evangelistic campaign in the village square. They sang joyfully in public, completely unbothered by the possibility of looking foolish—much like those we had seen on the steps of the Sacré-Coeur in Paris. Curious, we wondered what motivated these boys and girls to sacrifice their holidays and sing in the hot sun, all while exuding a happiness that didn't seem to rely on wine or any other indulgence.

We asked them what their secret was and they smiled warmly at us, answering, 'Jesus est vivant, Jesus is alive!' There was something about their conviction, the way they lived out their faith so freely, which stayed with me long after that encounter. It was unlike anything I had experienced before—an infectious joy that left me questioning my own understanding of happiness.

Italy

Since Vlieland, the islands have drawn me in with an irresistible magnetic force. We took a ferry to Porquerolles and on the beach, we encountered a young couple who generously offered us freshly caught fish, which they fried over a crackling wood fire. It saved us a meal, sharing wine from cardboard cups by the smouldering fire, while the couple spoke enthusiastically about *Jesus, le Seigneur.*

That night, lying on the beach beneath a clear starry sky, I wondered how this Jesus had inspired so many young people we met.

The next day, we toured triumphantly along the stunning French Riviera. We spent the nights in the gardens of abandoned villas, basking in the magnificent views over the bays. In Monaco, where illuminated yachts were floating serenely in the water, we felt invincible in our youthful freedom. Ton mused, 'Who's richer than us? The whole world belongs to us!'

Our idyllic journey hit a snag while riding on a rural road through the warm plains of the Po under the setting sun. A sharp sound rang out and the engine stalled. I found out there was no compression in the cylinder anymore and we had to push the bike, hoping to find a garage.

Out of nowhere, a little Fiat pulled up beside us and through the open window, a man asked, *'Cosa c'è?'* Pointing at the engine block, I replied, *'Mia macchina è rotta.'* The young man in blue overalls got out, knelt beside the bike and diagnosed the problem. Without consulting, he took a long rope from his car's trunk and tied one end to his rear bumper and the other to my bike's steering column. He signalled for Ton to sit with him in the car while he towed me on the bike for several kilometres.

We soon left the main road and bounced along a dirt track until we arrived at a large walled farmhouse. The young man introduced himself as Angelo and welcomed us into the world of his extended family—parents, grandparents, in-laws, siblings, and nieces and nephews. Then Angelo showed us a room on the first floor of an empty house within the farm complex, which smelled strongly of the pigs roaming freely below.

That evening, we enjoyed macaroni and abundant Chianti with the entire family in the warm, bustling kitchen. After dinner, Angelo took us to his garage where he hoisted my bike with chains. He disassembled the cylinder head and showed us a broken overhead valve that had pierced the piston. The necessary parts, including the head gasket, had to be ordered from Milan. Angelo asked if we wanted to wait for it.

'Si, si, prego,' I replied, grateful for his hospitality. Our unplanned stay with Angelo and his family gave us a glimpse of the warmth and generosity of rural Italy while we waited for the bike to be repaired.

On the farm, the gorgeous sisters of Angelo were busy and perhaps our mechanic hoped that we were potential marriage candidates. Unfortunately, these beauties spoke an Italian dialect and my years of classical Latin faltered miserably. How come, a few years earlier, I had communicated with a beautiful native girl during a holiday job on Lago di Garda in Italy?

After the engine was repaired, Angelo neatly welded the leaking fuel tank and exhaust pipe. As a farewell, our 'angel' showed us the red-light district of Milan in his little Fiat. Men dressed as women were the main attraction, which didn't interest us. The last breakfast was extensive and we got a hearty packed lunch from the Sorelle.

Arriving in Venice, it became noticeable that Ton started spending our household money generously, while we had just made a significant dent in our budget. Mr. Tourist enjoyed sitting on terraces in Venice and buying expensive newspapers while we were barely halfway.

The next evening, lying in a beautiful mountain meadow, Ton suddenly became 'homesick'. His 'planned holiday' seemed over and later, I found out that his military service time now had arrived. My 'friend', who had promised to travel around the world with me, had lied. I felt betrayed but didn't want to show it, the best way to hurt him was to act as though our friendship never existed. I said, 'Okay, I'll drop you off at the highway tomorrow morning and you can hitchhike home.' I turned over as if I wanted to sleep.

The next morning, I dropped Ton off at the highway and rode away without looking back.

Instead of feeling sad or depressed, I unexpectedly felt a sense of freedom. Free at last! With my yellow helmet strapped to the sissy bar, I cruised joyfully along the winding roads of the rocky coastline. My hair fluttered in the warm wind and I loudly sang Steppenwolf's song from the movie 'Easy Rider'.

'I can climb so high
I never wanna die
Born to be wild
Head out on the highway
Lookin' for adventure'

Athens

In former Yugoslavia, the landscape became more rugged. Gypsy children begged for money and they pelted me with stones when I refused to stop. Due to hypothermia and exhaustion, I skidded twice on the almost impassable mountain roads and one time, I balanced on the crankcase on a boulder at the edge of a gaping ravine. The euphoria of the newly won freedom faded in the looming fog.

For the night, I took cover behind a fence in a small forest. I hid in my waterproof sleeping bag as it began to drizzle. Shivering from the cold, I heard, in addition to the steady dripping, a sudden rustling and snorting, interspersed with the creaking of branches. Even the ground trembled and I expected an attack from a great beast but, it disappeared.

At the crack of dawn, I had finally dozed off, until a huge cow's head loomed above me. Nearly having a heart attack, I appreciated this beastly gesture as a funny greeting from Mr. Providence.

Descending into Greece was like sliding into a hot bath. At the Poste Restante in Athens, I found in addition to letters from my family, one postcard from Ton. Apparently, he wanted to make amends by arranging a meeting with his brother, a KLM steward who flew to Athens weekly.

Indeed, the meeting took place in front of the Parthenon on the Acropolis and dressed in jeans covered with oil stains, I followed the steward through the chic foyer of the Hilton Hotel in his suite. On behalf of his brother, he gave me 25 guilders and told me that Ton's luggage had been stolen that morning on the highway where I had dumped him. In addition, the holidaymaker had arrived just too late for his military service and had to wait months until the next intake. I feigned compassion even though I enjoyed the gloating. After a luxurious bath, I dressed in the smelly jeans that I had 'washed' and bleached in the sun at a deserted campsite along the coast outside Athens. The trousers had become stiff as leather, which many motorcyclists prefer.

In this idyllic yet lonely place, I spent the nights in the company of a large black dog covered in ticks around her eyes. I gave her some food in exchange for feeling safe during the dark hours.

Every day, a beautiful blonde arrived as she was dropped off at this place by two gentlemen in an expensive limousine. The car remained parked at a distance and the full-figured girl looked like the daughter of a wealthy shipping magnate. Unfortunately, she only spoke Greek and I still wonder what she saw in me, a filthy rover. While I sniffed her expensive perfume during the rides on the motorcycle, the gentle touch of her breasts against my back aroused me. I hoped to get rid of the black limousine by riding through the narrow streets of the villages along the coast, but I always brought her back to the shore on time, where she was once again collected.

An old Greek fisherman with white hair and dark eyes visited this spot daily as well and being a former immigrant from America, he spoke English very well. I asked him if he knew the book by Ernest Hemingway, 'The Old Man and the Sea'. It was required reading for my school list and yes he also loved tuna fishing. He shared his lunch of fresh bread with goat cheese, olives, and tomatoes. For hours, I enjoyed the conversation with this wise old man, who mentioned before he left, 'I have a tip for you, in downtown Athens, you can donate your blood and get well paid for it.' My first blood donation was not in a clean environment but it gave me free refreshments and enough money to buy a ticket for the ferry from Piraeus to Haifa on September 21, 1972.

STAGE 7

Israel

During the crossing to the Promised Land, the light was bright, as if something special was about to happen. On the large deck was always a fresh breeze and watching the seagulls from my sleeping bag, I felt incredibly happy, although I was a homeless drifter with no money.

I challenged a Thai girl to play chess on my little folding board and as I kept checkmating her, she always had to treat me to some tasty food. I tried to understand her motives and why she was paying me so much attention; she was too pretty and decent for me. 'Why do you play chess with me?'

Smiling, she pointed to the king piece on the chessboard. 'The Master Chess player is the King of the universe, and He wants you to be His friend.' 'Sorry, my dear, this **is** a bit out of the blue. Please explain.'

'The King of Kings is also the Man of Sorrows, who gave His life for you.'

Beyond that, the content escaped me completely because I was obsessed with her pure beauty. Nothing marred her, I could not discover a single flaw in her appearance. In addition to a perfect figure, her long, shiny hair framed her intelligent face with her large eyes. When she spoke, always smiling, she showed perfect teeth and her hushed voice had a sexy oriental accent. This delightful creature smelled of spikenard but, as she came, she flitted away like a butterfly.

At the end of that day, I stood at the railing as the ship approached the port of Rhodes. Coincidentally, I saw her disembark and, on the quay, in the crowd, she turned around and waved at me with a yellow scarf. How did she know I was watching her? Three more times, she turned around and waved exuberantly. I was deeply moved and wondered if she was an angel or a kind of alien.

During the night, I gazed at the brilliant starry dome and pondered her words. Why would the Creator of the vast universe want to be my friend? Why me, an insignificant ant-boy in a human heap?

After leaving Cyprus, I heard among the travellers a voice with a Dutch accent. It came from a young woman with an androgynous face, short light brown hair and a rotund figure. She looked at me with sparkling eyes and her name was Hannie, a medical student from Groningen. She was looking for a kibbutz and before disembarking in Haifa, I made a deal with her, I would take her to a suitable kibbutz if she would pay for gasoline and food.

I entered the Holy Land with only ten guilders and the Israeli customs officers asked if I had enough money to leave the country. I pointed to my motorcycle, but these port officials shook their heads disdainfully, considering the vehicle too dilapidated. They wanted to see some cash. Like a blind passenger, I searched in my pockets in vain and the men grew impatient as I was holding up the stream of travellers. As they were about to set me aside for the return trip, Hannie stepped forward with a flapping bundle of traveller's cheques.

On September 24, we set foot in the Holy Land. Hannie's backpack fit exactly on the gas tank again and we headed south along the coast. Mediterranean smells washed over us like warm waves of the sea and for a place to sleep, I chose the beach at Hadera, where two turtle doves cooed in a palm tree. The spot was very romantic until a coconut dropped next to my head. We shifted our sleeping bags further down towards the beach and during sunset, I began to feel like King Solomon. Hannie's mischievous eyes sparkled like diamonds before the rushing surf that rhythmically choreographed with the concert of the cicadas in the dunes. The moon should have stood still here as the sun once did for Joshua.

The next morning we left for Tel Aviv, where Hannie knew an immigrant Dutch couple who bred chinchillas. We stayed there for two nights on the scullery floor and heard about the harsh life of the average Jewish immigrant. The couple recommended Ginossar as the best kibbutz, beautifully situated along the Sea of Galilee. Kibbutzim were popular among globetrotters and volunteers were happy to come to help build up the country. You could taste the positive atmosphere of a pioneer state in the making. We toured through the Holy Land, which smelled of cedars, eucalyptus, pine trees and citrus groves full of oranges, lemons or grapefruit.

In Ginossar, they asked me and my fellow passenger about our marital status, which could not be substantiated. I had to share a room with a young Japanese guy. The next morning, Akihiko brought me to work in the banana jungle, where sturdy kibbutzniks with large machetes chopped off heavy bunches of bananas. We had to slog on our backs through the mud to a trailer pulled by a tractor.

At the end of September, it was still sweltering on these plantations, about a hundred fifty meters below sea level. While toiling with my Asian roommate, I remembered the movie 'The Bridge on the River Kwai', in which also Dutchmen from Indonesia were beaten up by Japanese soldiers. I also felt exploited and wondered what social system I hoped to find here. In contrast to the hard work, we were only given room and board, laundered work clothes and some pocket money for toothpaste or cigarettes. Every two months, the volunteers were invited to see the manufacture of wine at the nearby monastery. I hardly saw Hannie anymore as she worked on a fishing boat at night.

After my request, I transferred to the air-conditioned kitchen, where I had to wash pots and pans for eight hours daily. My fingertips were raw, thanks to the leaky rubber gloves. After a few weeks, I traded with a mate in the cotton fields, where you were supposed to tremble the white cotton balls in an iron container. At least you could converse with a buddy and exchange information about the hotspots in the world, waiting for the next load of cotton from the combiner. After the cotton harvest, I became an assistant to Mordechai, who nicknamed me Moshe. This pleasant, autistic guy with an angular head welded pipes together for irrigation around the kibbutz. Although he had warned me extensively not to look into the welding fire, I lay in bed for three days with hellish burning eyes. My ever-happy roommate took good care of me and compared me laughing to a certain 'Saul, who became Paul.' Akihiko never sat around the campfire with the other volunteers in the evening but consistently studied a large black book with weird Japanese characters. Later I discovered it was the Bible and at his farewell, I was deeply moved. This attentive young man, even after the hard work in the jungle, was always willing to care and clean up the room while humming psalms.

I took some days off to prove myself by walking around the Sea of Galilee. I couldn't walk on the water yet, but I believed everybody could become like Christ with consistent meditation. The walk is feasible within a few days if you have sufficient drinks and food, which I forgot about. Starting on the west side in the sun, I was already very thirsty after a few kilometres.

Everywhere in the Holy Land are 'holy site shields', with explanatory texts mentioning mostly Biblical events. Here I read that Jesus had fed five thousand people with two fish and five loaves of bread.

I didn't want to drink the water from the lake because it looked like foamed from chemicals. With miles to go, I thought of the miraculous feeding and I shouted to Providence to arrange me some water.

Behold, a stone's throw away, a litre bottle of grapefruit juice, with the label almost loose, was lying in the rippling waves of the lake. 'What a coincidence!' While greedy drinking, I walked on and saw barely a hundred meters away, two naked men bathing. Politely they turned their backs towards me. So it was not a coincidence? They put the bottle to cool it!

I strode and wondered about this mysterious happening. Was it Providence who provided or the two men? Or is it both? Is Providence an intelligent being? I remembered a quote from Einstein, 'Coincidence is God's way of remaining anonymous.'

When I returned to Ginossar, Hannie had taken the place of the Japanese roommate without consulting me. She was expecting me to be elated by her surprise, but I wasn't happy, because we didn't have a real relationship. To the volunteers, we now looked like a couple but I had Karin from Sweden in mind, who lived opposite in the 'ghetto'. She began to ignore me, like in a true soap opera.

In the meantime, I was promoted to the official garbageman and allowed to drive the tractor 'Cougar'. I owed this job to Tom from Toronto who taught me to swear in English.

Early in the morning, I collected first the milk cans at the 'dairy' to deliver them in a trailer to the kitchen. Then I had to lift all the containers one by one in the kibbutz with a hydraulic system and empty them on the dump, close to the lake.

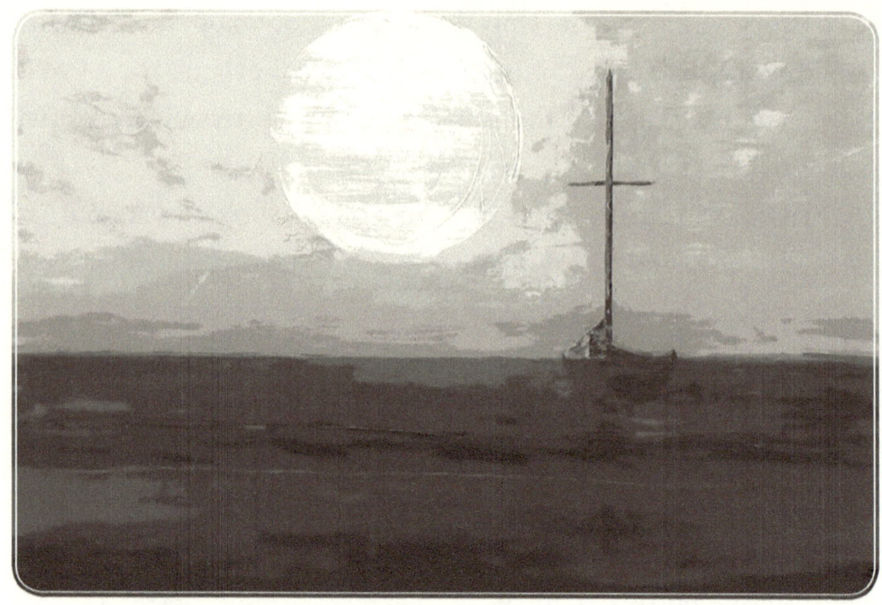

Sea of Galilea

There I had plenty of time to spot stray pelicans, ospreys, kingfishers, bee-eaters and a few hoopoes. Israel is a pre-eminent overflight route above the pivot point between Europe, Asia, and Africa, a veritable El Dorado for ornithologists.

Normally, it took eight hours to empty all the bins, but I noticed that most were only half full or empty. Since the temperature was dropping in November, the bins were smelling less and I tried to empty them every other day from now on. It saved me four hours of driving. I hid Cougar among the eucalyptus trees near the ghetto and took a sun chair on the large restaurant terrace by the lake. Karin, the waitress at the Ginossar guesthouse, provided me with a free beer. I didn't feel like being exploited anymore, reading my favourite book, 'The world perishes by too much labour', by Max Dendermonde. 'Lechaim, cheers'! I toasted to Karin, the Swedish beauty I spotted from the beginning. Our relationship grew steadily until she discovered my acute concubinage with Hannie. I apologized profusely that the initiative did not come from my side but Karin distrusted me and the kibbutzniks questioned about my long stay in work clothes on the terrace, where only paying hotel guests used to sit. Cougar was tracked down in the bush, after which a social sanction followed. I had to spend the remaining four hours in the dusty poultry shed, where thousands of ugly, clucking chickens were waiting to be vaccinated.

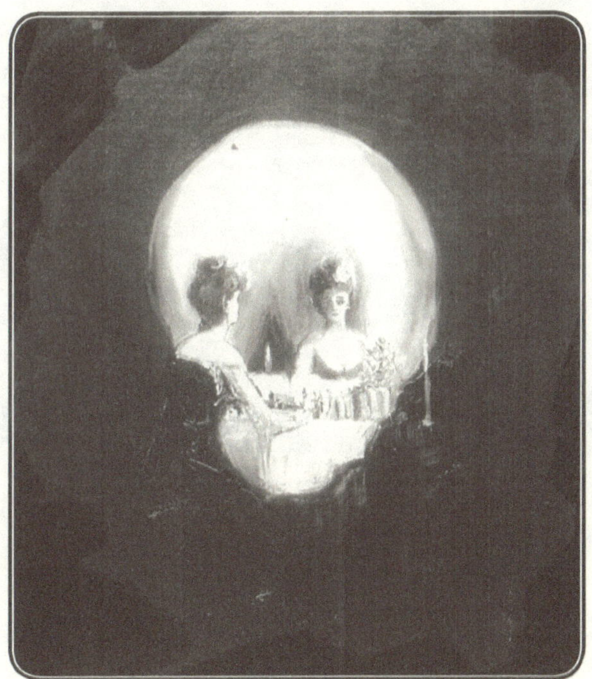

All is vanity

The motif in my favourite book that most in life is vanity, kept bubbling up in my mind and why couldn't I be satisfied with my easy eight-hour job? Why always rub against the grain of life? I could easily have grown old here. 'Better a handful of rest than both fists full of the torment of the spirit', Max quoted from Ecclesiastes.

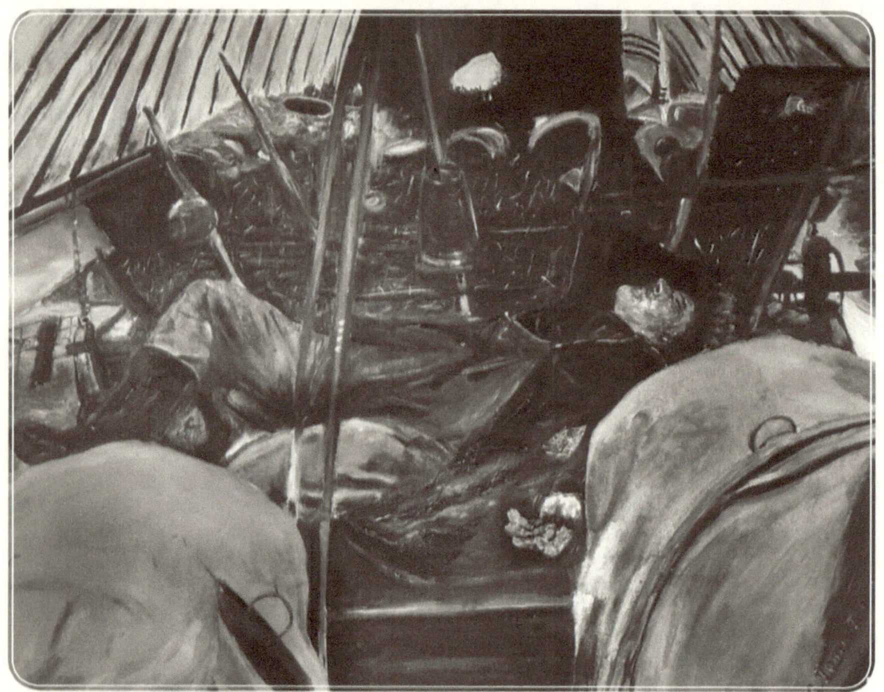

A handful of rest

Why couldn't I find peace? Why my torment from the turmoil of searching for the most existential question in life? What is the meaning of it all? Is everything vanity and meaningless? Nobody could give me a satisfying answer in my search for truth.

I had ticked off Christianity and recently also Islam. Driving through the Holy Land, I could distinguish the Palestinian Muslim villages from miles away by the car wrecks or ruins along the road. The Muslim quarter in Jerusalem differed considerably in cleanliness from the Jewish, Christian, or Armenian sections. You know the tree by its fruits, once a famous rabbi stated.

Will I find the truth in India, the so-called land of wisdom? How can I leave Israel without money? The degraded motorbike would not bring in enough finances.

A volunteer told me that in nearby Beth Shean, I could earn thirty Israeli pounds a day in shooting a movie entitled 'Jesus Christ Superstar'. Maybe they would allow me to participate and travel with the crew to different locations.

I rode my iron donkey to the film set and at that moment, they were filming the scene of Jesus before Herod. Again and again, the crew had to chant, 'Crucify, crucify! I could have earned thirty pounds that day, but I remembered from school the thirty pieces of silver Judas received for his betrayal. I respected hippie Jesus too much to shout, 'Crucify Him' over and over again.

Was the experience with the grapefruit bottle by the lake that forced me to make a radical U-turn? Years later, I would see this musical with amazing music, but unfortunately, Jesus is portrayed as a dreamy loser. Was He not in total control of His life? Years later in 2011, I was on the market square in Gouda, where the musical The Passion for the first time was performed and in response to Pilate's question as to who should be released, the audience had to shout three times, 'Barabbas.' A feeling of déjà vu rose within me and I refused.

Among the volunteers, there was a rumour that one could earn tax-free money in Eilat at the Red Sea. How could I ride to southern Israel without petrol?

I bought a crate of wine bottles at the monastery next door to treat my ghetto fellows at the campfire and meanwhile, I shared my problem with the group. Ulrich, a Swiss hippie with blond, long, straight hair, offered to escort me with his scooter during the trip through the desert. He even wanted to support me for a few days in Eilat and if necessary, we would ride back together.

In mid-December, I said farewell to Karin and Hannie and promised to return within a week if I didn't find a job, otherwise, I would write letters. Karin was just like Gaby, my ideal woman with natural streaks in her blond hair. Carol King's song, 'You've Got a Friend' in winter, spring, summer, or fall, still reminds me of her. I would visit her in Sweden and would write many letters she never answered, probably being intercepted by her parents.

After a spectacular trip through the Negev desert, the nights were bitterly cold on the beach of Eilat. We lived on coffee, falafel, shawarma, oranges and wine. Every morning at six o'clock, I was present on the terrace of 'Charley's Point' where contractors in their pick-ups drove by to select labourers, just like in old biblical times.

On the third day, I was picked out of the group by a foreman from the 'Ashdrome' company, together with a Danish boy, called Christian. We were taken to a large construction site, where a small shed with three bunk beds would be our future residence. I would live there for six weeks with three Palestinians, an American student and the ruddy Dane Christian. During the first days, we had to cut holes in reinforced concrete which caused muscle pain and blisters. Then we had to clear concrete formwork. Thanks to an advance from the foreman, I survived the first week on falafels, shawarma or what the Palestinians gave me from their cooking on a butane gas set. In the evening we all lay exhausted, like animals in a stable. I could leave again after a few weeks or months, but the Palestinians would stay as it was their way of living.

Suddenly, a ghost appeared in the doorway and I was shocked because this woman was my mother. Once I recovered, I faked joy and it surprised me how quickly I automatically settled into the role of the well-behaved son. Mrs. Tompot had chosen Israel for her Christmas holiday and during the days in the Ginossar Guesthouse, she had inquired about Maurits Tompot. A beautiful Swedish girl had told her that Moshe travelled to Eilat on his motorbike. After visiting Bethlehem and Jerusalem for Christmas, Mother had booked a week in a B & B in Eilat. On the streets, she had asked people about a young Dutchman on a motorbike. During my daily trips to the food stool, I had attracted attention with the loose exhaust pipe, which backfired due to the dysregulated ignition.

During the coming holiday of New Year, I could take a few days off and finally shower and wash clothes in my mother's room. She booked bus trips to Solomon's mines in the desert and the deep-sea aquarium along the Red Sea. On the bus she constantly tried to keep the conversation going, while I dozed off in the sun behind the window. She kept asking questions about my faith until I exclaimed, 'Please stop it! I have nothing with your religion! If I've ruined your Christmas holidays, so be it. I didn't ask you to come, did I?' This was probably like a dagger in her heart, but her moist eyes when she departed made an impression on me; on the contrary, I was glad she left.

The foreman took Christian and me to a pile of rebar which had been tipped off a truck. The mess of iron bars and rods with arches had to be sorted and the manager asked how long we needed to sort this out.

'A few weeks probably.'

The boss laughed loudly, 'No gentlemen, a few days should be enough.'

'Okay, we'll fix it in one week.'

The foreman agreed and the deal was made for a full week's work. We tried to get the job done sooner. We were then paid the agreed amount and could start the next job. This so-called 'kabbalah nout system' made us a team of draft horses which developed me into a bodybuilder.

Our efforts pleased the supervisor so much that he asked us to work as paid labourers in a nearby kibbutz, Yotvata. This was the jackpot; in addition to salary, housing and clean sanitary facilities, free food was included!

During the first weeks, we behaved like gluttons, devouring the ample food provided after two months of substandard rations.

In the desert, we were given the honourable task of digging pits for picket posts. Under the comfortable winter sun, after the abundant midday meals, we could not resist the temptation to take long siestas in the self-dug pits. After a first warning, the foreman found us asleep a second time and the third time we were discharged on the spot. Honestly, we were fed up with this work and I had earned more than two hundred dollars. I could leave Israel, but where could I exchange my Israeli pounds? No bank in the country or abroad would exchange the Israeli money. I had heard of a monastery in Galilee and Christian would also travel north. I asked him if he wanted to ride with me to Tel Aviv and he nodded. 'Would you mind riding back around the Sinai desert with me?' He shrugged.

Up to Sharm el-Sheikh, we steamed briskly until a sign appeared with a text in Arabic, Hebrew and English: 'No trespassing military area'. We decided not to understand the text and continued to hum along with a full tank of petrol.

After 350 kilometres, halfway along the road to El Arish, the roar of the engine died down to an ear-numbing silence in the undulating sea of sand.

Christian broke the silence with a loud curse and he grabbed his backpack, took one of the two cans of cola and drifted down the endless road.

Strangely enough, I didn't care that he left. I experienced an unexpected peace, that special feeling of being alone in a remote place, like being the first on the beach in the morning or skating on a frozen lake. I felt a holy awe in this great emptiness.

Spontaneously, I began to speak in English to the God of Israel who he helped me at the Sea of Galilee. He led His people through this wilderness providing them with water and food.

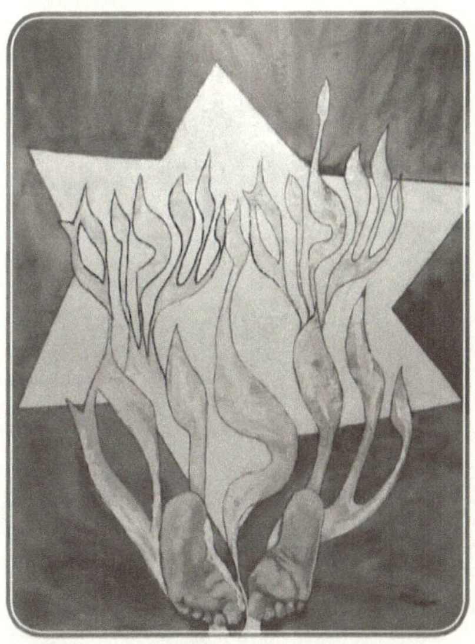

Tripple peace

After a little prayer, I saw a cloud of dust as big as one man's fist. A Jeep with four Israeli soldiers was toiling through the loose dirt in my direction. They might have spotted us a while ago and as they jumped out of the vehicle, the commander started to yell at me that I was in a forbidden area. I shrugged and pointed at my tank, saying, 'Sorry sir, no understand, no petrol!

He nodded to one of his men, who grabbed a jerry can from behind the vehicle and poured litres of gasoline into my tank.

'Now, get the hell out of here!'

Fortunately, the BMW started directly and a few kilometres further on the road, I picked up Christian. He didn't care how I had done this, but I felt like Moses who had just seen a burning bush. The Thai girl said that God can be your friend and I started to sing Carole King›s song aloud,

> 'You just call out my name
> And you know wherever I am
> I'll come running to see you again
> Winter, spring, summer or fall
> All you have to do is call
> And I'll be there
> You've got a friend.'

A bizarre trip past ghost towns and destroyed army tricks followed. In completely deserted villages along the Red Sea, curtains still fluttered in the house windows. Sailboats were on the shore and barbers' chairs stood as if they had been abandoned yesterday.

Exactly with the last drop of fuel, we reached El Arish and as if in the old Levant, we wandered around in the covered market, full of stalls with colourful goods on display. Fragrant herbs were piled up like small pyramids next to piles of nuts, fabric, clothes, household items and even gold or what looked like it. Being the only tourists, we were offered coffee and tea everywhere.

Arriving in the centre of Tel Aviv, artists invited us to stay at their exhibition, due to my roaring chopper at the entrance. It resulted in a place to sleep with an older artist. He turned out to be gay and thought we had to have a sexual experience with him, a homosexual. We didn't think it was appropriate and remained awake that night.

Netofa

The next morning, Christian and I parted ways. I travelled to Galilee and found the village of Deir Hanna, from where a very steep rocky road led to the monastery. Although the simple settlement of Netofa consisted of a row of barracks, it had a very unique view in Israel. To the west, the blue Mediterranean Sea was shining and to the east, the azure Sea of Galilee shimmered.

I met two elderly, bearded monks, the American Tom and the Dutchman Jacob Willebrands. They coached a group of globetrotters and recently, a young Jewish South African arrived. He was willing to become a novice and Neville spoke funny Afrikaans to me. He resembled the Jesus from the children's Bibles, with blue eyes and long, blond curly hair. Tom and Jacob were delighted with his arrival since he attracted young people and the monastery seemed to flourish like the Rose of Sharon.

As crew members, we worked in the mornings in the chapel cave or on the rocky road. In the afternoon, everyone was free, except the young Canadian Mary, who meditated early in the morning and ran the household. After the evening meal, one of the monks opened the Holy Scripture to read. It caused often political discussions with a Palestinian, almost anti-Israeli attitude.

One afternoon, I took the donkey for a ride over the hills and to take a rest, I lay in the grass, enjoying the splendid panorama. The donkey grazed quietly close to me and larks sang as a sweet delight. I thought of unsaddling the donkey with its burden for a while. Once freed, the animal pricked up its big ears and jumped around me in wide circles. That was beautiful to see, but finally, it trotted out of sight.

Sweating from dragging the saddle, I reached the monastery and when I explained what happened, Thomas asked scornfully, 'Who is now the donkey or Jackass?'

A few days later, the jack-of-all-trades, Nevill, was tipped off by villagers; they had spotted the donkey and lured it with food.

Maybe because I was Dutch, Jacob asked me to drive him in the Land Rover to Jerusalem, where he had to attend a conference. The monk was now dressed as a priest in a black cassock and as we arrived, he soon dissolved into a procession of other religious people in black on the Via Dolorosa. I classified them as a theatrical performance of Pharisees and hypocrites. I bet Jesus was different.

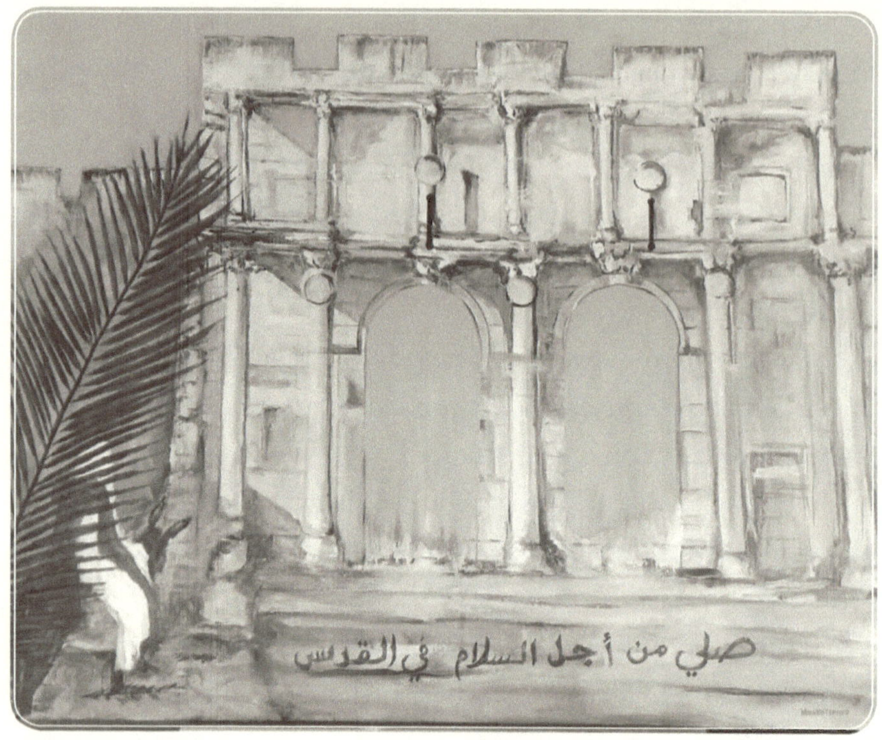

Golden Gate

On the spot, my plan to visit India was decided and toasted with a cold beer on a terrace. Was it Karl Marx, a Jew, who said that religion is like opium to the people? I had not found my spiritual satisfaction in the monastery and if India didn't bring what I was looking for, Australia or New Zealand would become my ultimate destination. The best option was to live in a commune somewhere down under, beekeeping and starting a weed plantation.

During one of my last days in Netofa, Neville had a surprise as a farewell in store. The novice had obtained LSD pills, which Jacob and Thomas didn't know. The pills had to be taken on an empty stomach, but I thought it was too suspicious that everyone would 'fast' that evening. So I had dinner with Tom, Jacob and Mary. Later I joined the group in the sleeping quarters and not knowing that you could not take such a pill after a meal, I ended up on a 'bad trip' or nightmare. The young playing kittens became ravening tigers and I fled outside, but now the stiff bushes with claws wanted to pull me into the underworld.

In the setting sun, Neville slowly became the devil himself and his shady cronies floated around me, trying to lure me to hell, which was the setting sun behind them. After the food was digested, the bad trip became a good trip and I ascended to the heavenly realms. Now Neville appeared to change into Christ with His disciples. Everything turned into a paradise but deep down, I realised it was all fake, a dream world. Days, weeks, months and even years later, momentary shooting stars flashed in my mind's eye. This powerful chemical seemed to damage my brain.

At the beginning of March, the temperature seemed pleasant enough to travel further. With Tom, I could exchange my Israeli money for a $220 check from Barclays Bank, New York. I had to assume that this little piece of paper could be cashed anywhere in the world. What faith can do—trusting a little piece of paper.

I gifted my motorbike to Neville to use for small errands in addition to the donkey and as thanks, he brought me in the Land Rover to Haifa, where I embarked on March 5, 1973.

Turkey

According to my old passport, I arrived in Cyprus on March 6 and left again on March 9, the day of my 21st birthday. On the boat, between Famagusta and Mersin in Turkey, I treated myself to duty-free whisky.

In Mersin, fake student cards were offered, allowing you to buy a train ticket for only twelve dollars bringing you to the Iranian border in three days. Corrupt officials always tried to ask for extra money, but I consulted with other travellers. I shared the train compartment with a German couple who had smoking as their hobby. They constantly changed brands at specific times of the day and talked extensively about the quality, cost, taste, smell, and type of filter. Throughout the entire train journey, Turks stared at us as if we were aliens.

In Iran most hippies with strong, patchouli-like smells transferred from trains to buses. In Afghanistan, cheap chunks of hashish flew through the bus as if they were gingerbread. On this hippie trail, joints or hash pipes were constantly being passed around, keeping me chronically stoned.

The consequences of hard drugs were visible in Kabul, where junkies were dying in the gutter and no one cared about them. Luggage was never safe, so I always used my bag as a pillow.

In the border area with Pakistan, hemp grew luxuriously along the road, like cow parsley at home. If I rubbed some of the buds in my hands and mixed the scrapings with the tobacco in my cigarette, I would be 'high' for hours. Sometimes I longed to be 'clean' again.

At the youth hostel in Lahore, I was approached by two friendly guys who tried to persuade me to take a free shot of heroin. 'You need to experience this once in your lifetime,' they said and after rolling up my sleeve, they tied a band around my arm to insert the hypodermic needle into the swollen vein. The image of the junkies in Kabul suddenly appeared in my mind and I fended off the syringe, saying, 'No, no, please stop it!

After my refusal, their kindness disappeared quickly and they rushed off to find their next victim for their drug trafficking.

In the cities of Pakistan, I became paranoid of the huge crowds and the endless calls to prayer from the countless speakers of the minarets.

A pivotal moment was a meeting with a sturdy, handsome Dutchman who rode from Australia on his Triumph motorcycle. With this hero, I exchanged my leather motorcycle jacket for a good meal and much travel advice about Down Under, the place to be. If India didn't offer what I was searching for, Australia would surely become my ultimate destination.

STAGE 8

India

Compared with Pakistan, India was a spiritual relief—unless you ended up in the hell of Old Delhi. In the scorching heat, deformed and handicapped people moved through the mud on handcrafted carts in between the skinny, so-called sacred cows.

I was bouncing into a culture shock. Was this superimposed misery the bitter fruit of Hinduism with its horrible caste system? I seriously started to doubt whether I would find what I was looking for here.

Before I left New Delhi, I picked up the coveted visas for Nepal at the embassy. Like Goa Beach, Kathmandu was a kind of terminus on the hippie trail.

From then on, I travelled on foot or hitchhiked with every available means of transportation. Sometimes I spent the night on hard stone sidewalks with a sheet as protection against insects and my little bag as a pillow.

In rural Punjab, I spent a night talking to a young guru dressed only in a loincloth. He lived in a shabby hut and we talked about truth, wisdom and the meaning of life. He asked me for example, 'Why do you assume that life has a purpose?'

I answered that I hated meaninglessness.

'Suppose there's a goal, it must have been set by someone, right?' he asked.

'Do you mean an Intelligence, a God or something?'

'Yes, we call them Brahma, Shiva, and Vishnu. You call it the Trinity, don't you? We have a lot in common, don't we?' He laughed.

'Indeed, but suppose that deity has set a goal, can we miss that destiny or fail in life?'

'Yes, but we first need to know who the deity is and what his deal is.'

We philosophised like this until the new day dawned with a unique sunrise and the sound of a rooster crowing. The guru appeared to be a sincere searching soul like me, yet he was venerated as a saint and fed by the village community as they brought him breakfast, which we enjoyed together.

After saying goodbye with a hug as good friends, I continued my journey between the wheat fields where locals knelt before me with folded hands, as if before the guru. Was his holiness radiating from me? I greeted them, but kneeling the same way. Gloom swept over me because I sincerely hoped that this man would have told me the truth and he didn't. A searching soul like me could also pretend to be a guru, I mused.

I strolled or hitched a ride with cyclists, ox-carts, cars or packed local buses while most Indian men were happy to ask the same questions all the time to practice their school English, 'Do you speak English? Are you married? Do you have children?' One particular hitchhike turned out to be catastrophic.

Uttar Pradesh

Along the road to Uttar Pradesh, I rubbed some of the tops of weed plants into the tobacco of my hand-rolled cigarette and smoked. While hitchhiking, a light blue truck with bells and whistles stopped in front of me as I raised my hand. The young driver and co-driver beckoned me into the cab, where I offered them my joint. Both men inhaled deeply and at the next toll stop, I asked if I was allowed to sit on top of the cab in the box. There was no noise and heat but a lovely breeze.

To my horror, the driver ignored the toll booth in the next village. He crashed through the barrier with a loud bang and thundered at full speed. I was shocked. did the driver get stoned because of my joint?

At an intersection, people were leisurely talking, but because of the high speed of the truck, they could barely flee. A stationary motorcyclist saw no chance of escape and was run over. From the box, I looked back and saw the man lying under his motorcycle. At the next toll booth, the road was blocked by trucks, forcing the driver to stop.

He and his co-driver were ordered to get out and taken at gunpoint. With their hands behind their heads, they had to sit on the ground.

Carefully, I emerged from the box and hesitantly approached the pair to sit next to them, but the driver gestured to me to keep walking. I will never forget his sad, dark look. This Indian took the blame when, in fact, I had caused this accident.

Was the motorcyclist dead, or would he become an invalid? Was the man married, did he have children? How much jail time would the driver serve?

With these thoughts, I trudged along, carrying a heavy backpack of regret. What were the consequences of this act on my karma? I would never use drugs again after this darkest page in my life.

When I arrived in Amritsar, I noticed that volunteers were cleaning their famous temple and most of them looked at me strangely when I joined the long line of pilgrims for the free food distribution. The last few weeks, I had only eaten chapatis and hot curry and at night my mouth watered when I thought of sandwiches with peanut butter or sprinkles. Dreams of sandwiches and minced meatballs filled my mind.

In the holy and hot city of Rishikesh, I knocked on the doors of several ashrams, which served as monasteries, hoping for some hospitality. But in the eyes of the pious gurus, only dollar signs were flickering. They asked a fee of at least $25 to be admitted to 'their enlightenment'.

The only coolness to be found was along the banks of the Ganges River, which flows from the Himalayas. My money had now dwindled to a handful of rupees because banks wouldn't change my check unless I waited at least eight weeks to cash it. For a few rupees, I found shelter on a site surrounded by high fencing, with only loose sand and no shade. A donkey was walking around with a dark stripe in her fur along her back and the only water came from a tap in a toilet cubicle, meant to wash your buttocks. There was another crazy hippie, who was watching the sun all day to get high. He was completely insane, and so was I, drinking the tap water, which resulted in severe diarrhoea.

Weakened, I stumbled in the intense heat to the Ganges to cool off. On the way, I became paranoid when sacred monkeys attacked me while defending their babies. I fended them off with my little bag, which they bit or clung to.

After a few days, I felt so weak that I thought I was going to die. I didn't expect any help from the hippies, although their slogan was 'peace and no war'; they all lived for themselves, just like me. Most Indians were too poor to care for others and they believed that dying is being born again. The result is that human life is worth nothing. I didn't see any bright light anymore, except the stars at night and I wondered if the God of Israel, could help me here in faraway India as well?'

The next day at the Ganges, I knelt along the shore and stammered only three words, 'God, help me!'

Stumbling back, I crossed paths with a German hippie. The young man with his long blond hair and a short dark brown beard looked at me disdainfully as if I were a leper. 'You look bad, man.'

Nodding I pointed to my stomach, saying, ‹Yes I feel bad, horrible.'

'Do you have dysentery?'

I shrugged and a little tube box emerged from his shoulder bag. 'Here, take two of those black pills with water from my bottle and from now on, only drink chai or tea, okay? I've just come from Mussoorie where I met some good people. They might have a place for you to recover. Salvation Army, I think, but cool people. They're guaranteed to help you.' This sounded like music to my ears, the goodwill of the Salvation Army was well-known to me.

'Please ask for the missionary man Stan in the Bible shop in Mussoorie, okay?' From his bag, he took a box of oil tubes and wrote on the back, 'For Stan, sincerely yours, Michael. Please give this to Mr. Hawthorne, okay? I won't be painting in this scorching heat and it saves me to carry it.'

Mussoorie

Thanks to the pills, I could hitchhike to Mussoorie the next day without nausea. Everything went extremely well and slowly the road led up to cool, green hills as if I arrived in heavenly spheres. Ferns grew on tree trunks and cheeky monkeys jumped on the roof of the bus.

Mussoorie was an old colonial resort, where the British used to spend the hot summers. The buildings were orderly with many trees in an attractive setting. I found the Bible shop and upon opening the door, a bell rang. A full-figured, beautiful woman appeared and welcomed me warmly as if she was expecting me. Her aura of love made me recoil like a pariah, I couldn't bear this overwhelming affection.

Was it because of my months of emotional isolation? Again she surprised me by questioning if I would like a cup of tea with a piece of cake.

'I received it this morning in the mailbox from my mother in Australia. Here, smell it, this time with vanilla and lemon, delicious isn't it!' I smelled it from a distance sitting on a tea chest at the entrance. Then the grand dame reached out and touched my hand to shake it. She introduced herself as Mary Hawthorne, wife of Stan and she apologised that her husband wasn't home yet, 'He will arrive any moment!'

She poured the chai, with lots of milk and sugar. The warm hospitality made me shudder, but I succumbed, drooling over the cake.

I showed the oil painting tubes to Stan as the so-called reason for my arrival. I also mentioned that I was looking for the philosophical meaning of life. Mary confided in a whisper that she had friends further up the mountain, where I might be able to stay.

In order not to sound too eager, I told her that I would stay at a hotel in the village and come back the next morning if her husband would be present.

'I will surely make him wait for you, Morris.'

To underline my good intentions, I bought a discounted King James Bible with my last rupees as a thank you. I had already spotted a simple hostel beforehand, a room with eight beds, equipped with wooden frames and braided rope as a mattress.

The next morning, a beaming Stan was waiting for me in the Bible shop. The tall, ruddy man received me warmly, although he was difficult to understand because of his Irish or Scottish accent. I thought it would be wise to mention that I had nowhere to cash my US check and Stan said that he would help me with his bank account. First, he asked kindly, but firmly, 'Do you know Jesus as your personal Savior?' I had no idea what he meant by this.

'Well, I heard of Jesus Christ Superstar recently', I answered.

'Okay, we'll talk about it later. Are you ready to see our brother Peter and sister Dorothy now? Let's go!'

We hiked up the ridge to Hamilton House, where Peter and Dorothy were waiting on the porch. The view from there was majestic. To the right, the planes stretched as far as the eye could see and to the left, the snow-capped Himalayan peaks.

Dorothy looked a lot like Mary, who was also blonde. Both women turned out to be Australian and Peter was of British-Indian descent, looking like a sporty Frank Zappa. I arrived emaciated, dressed in green-yellow, striped, pyjama-like clothes, with a ponytail and only my small bag.

After getting acquainted with the usual chai, the couple showed me a room where I could stay. Back on the terrace, Stan asked, 'Do you like Hamilton House?'

'Of course, I loved it!'

Stan said goodbye after expressing the hope to meet and greet again at the church the coming Sunday. 'My beloved wife, Mary, will sing a solo in the service and we hope that you will soon come to know Jesus as your personal Lord and Savior.'

That same day, Peter gave me a book entitled '*God's Smuggler*' by Anne van der Bijl. This Dutch missionary smuggled Bibles to the countries behind the Iron Curtain. The next weeks, I would spend hours reading in a rocking chair on the porch in front of the immense, spacious, heavenly sky changing by the second. Despite the onset of the monsoon with curtains of rain, I experienced an unprecedented tranquillity and felt I had come home.

I did not feel at home at all in the Methodist church with the happy-clappy people, despite the songs Mary sang in devotion with her little harp, '*Surely goodness and mercy shall follow me, all the days of my life.*'

Dorothy cooked tastefully and her desserts, especially the home-baked pastry with hot custard, were excellent. Another guest, a young Canadian Jesuit priest, joined us for dinner and it was amusing that he kept criticising what Peter preached at the table. This priest did not take the Scriptures seriously and after the meal, when the Bible was opened to read a chapter, it often led to heated discussions.

After the first meal, the chapter was about the prodigal son and I felt their gaze was directed at me but I felt more like a drifter who had washed up here due to circumstances. Was it my fault that the banks in India worked so slowly and the tap water made you sick? At that moment then the hitchhiking accident flashed through my mind, I was more than a prodigal son, a possible murderer was sitting here at the supper table.

On the second evening, Peter read the fascinating story of the Good Samaritan.

I had ridden that same desolate road in the wilderness from Jericho to Jerusalem, with the crackle of a loose exhaust pipe echoing off the bare hills. I could easily imagine how, in this godforsaken environment, black-clad orthodox people would just walk by, while a Palestinian would take care of the victim. I identified Peter with the Good Samaritan but he emphatically pointed to Jesus as the Merciful One, who wants to carry us on His donkey. 'Do you know that donkeys have a narrow strip of darker hair running down their back and across their shoulders? This naturally makes the shape of a cross. Do you think this is a coincidence?'

I shrugged, even though I had only ever seen one stripe.

A few days later, I received another book, 'The Late Great Planet Earth' by Hal Lindsey. The cover of this bestseller highlighted how ancient Bible prophecies were being fulfilled and although I didn't like American bestsellers, my curiosity was piqued by this one. Lindsey wrote that the greatest sign of God could be seen in the Jewish people, particularly in how they were returning to the Promised Land. With my own eyes, I had seen the pioneer state taking shape, the only democracy in the Middle East since the Declaration of Independence in 1948.

The rabbi from Nazareth had walked around Palestine for three years and before His farewell to His disciples, He foretold His return with the re-establishment of the Jewish nation. Was the existence of the Jewish nation demonstrable proof of God's existence?

I noticed a lot of Tibetans in Mussoorie and asked Peter if they came to visit the Dalai Lama, who lived in the nearby village of Dehradun. 'No, they are all exiles, like the Dalai Lama himself. Don't you know that China has annexed Tibet?'

No, but I realised this was also a serious sign, a prophecy from the Book of Revelation since the Chinese are restoring the ancient Silk Road, across the Himalayas towards the West. Peter showed the prophesy that one day an army of 200 million soldiers will march out of the land of the rising sun towards the West and only one country can produce such a massive army. Other nations will also gather in Israel, which will cause the great catastrophic clash at Armageddon.

I was shocked as a whole new perspective opened up for me. I vaguely knew of the Club of Rome, founded by European scientists concerned about the world's future. Barry McGuire's song 'Eve of Destruction' was familiar to me, but this was breaking news—the entire end-times scenario had been predicted thousands of years ago.

I challenged Peter with the question, 'Is the Bible prophecy necessary to predict how things will turn out? If another madman like Hitler comes up, history will repeat itself. The only difference now is the presence of a nuclear arsenal.'

'Exactly,' Peter replied. 'Two thousand years ago, nobody knew about atomic bombs and yet their power is described in the

Apocalypse. God knows how it ends and He wants to warn and comfort us, just as Jonah was instructed to do.'

'What do you mean by 'comforting us?' I asked.

'Well, God warned and spared Nineveh and if Jesus will not intervene, mankind will completely exterminate itself.'

All this information made me dizzy, I needed a walk.

Over seven weeks, I studied hundreds of prophecies and the possibility that the Bible was correct grew stronger by the day. Some prophecies were easy to fulfil, like the one in Zechariah, 'Behold, your King is coming to you, meek and seated on a donkey.' Jesus asked His disciples to borrow a donkey from a nearby village on which He entered Jerusalem, a simply self-fulfilling prophecy.

Peter answered, 'Exactly, but tell me, what king comes on a donkey colt? Usually, a monarch rides a large white horse, accompanied by an imposing retinue that radiates power. What other people on Earth have such an honest history book as the Old Testament? Practically all the heroes go astray—yes, even the richest and wisest King Solomon.'

This gave me a lot to think about. The entry into Jerusalem on a donkey was easy enough to arrange, but determining the place of your birth, like being born in Bethlehem, is entirely different and difficult. Micah had prophesied, 'But you, Bethlehem Ephrathah, though you are small among the clans of Judah, out of you will come for me one who will be ruler over Israel, whose origins are from of old, from ancient times.'

At Jesus' death on the cross, hundreds of prophecies were fulfilled like all the sacrifices of the Old Testament—from the smallest dove to the largest bull—pointing to His ultimate sacrifice. His life had been predicted in detail and abundantly foreshadowed by figures like Moses, Samson, Jonah, Joseph, and many others.

I discovered that the Bible is a monument like the Pyramid of Giza, standing the test of time for centuries. Peter challenged me with this statement, 'When Jesus says He is the Truth, He is either the Truth or the greatest liar. What do you think, you agree? Check it out yourself—it's a fifty-fifty chance.'

I had already passed the fifty mark and was approaching an eureka moment, as if I was standing on the pyramid, looking over centuries of history. The rejected cornerstone was the Stone of Emissions, the Rock of Annoyance, the Rock of all Ages—I had been searching for or did He finally find me?

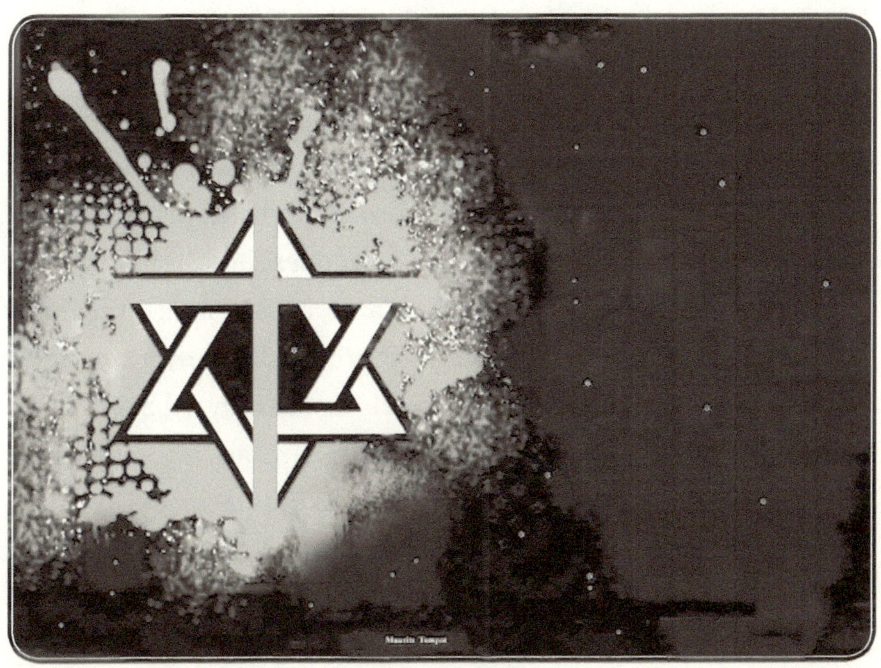

Eureka

Enthusiastically, I began sending letters home, telling them that I found in India what I had been looking for. The last postcard I sent from Kabul showed an Afghan man smoking a 'chilm,' a type of pipe used for hashish. After months of silence, my family was relieved to know I was still alive. My letters now were filled with Bible verses, leading them to suspect I had become involved in a cult.

One phrase from the Gospel kept echoing in my mind like a mantra, 'Seek first my kingdom and my righteousness and I will give you everything.'

Due to Peter's open prayer time at the table, I too, began 'talking' to God during my walks in the hills around Mussoorie. 'What do you mean by everything, Lord?'

To me, 'everything' included my journey around the world.

I slowly began to understand that Christianity is not a religion of rules, but a relationship with Him, the One who wants the best for you. The Bible is about Jesus, the Word of God and just as human beings communicate through words, so does God. Jesus is not a vague Providence but a Person with a name—Yeshua—meaning 'Yahweh is the Savior.' His Word was written down over centuries by various 'secretaries,' and wittily, He is the only ancient writer who still lives. You can talk and walk with Him, ask questions, give thanks, and build up a relationship. Like Adam in the Garden, I walked through the thickly wooded hills and tried to listen to that Voice, meditating on the mantra, 'Seek my Kingdom first and everything shall be added to you.'

I heard another voice whispering like the leaves. 'Don't forget the unused stamp in your passport, my friend!'

Soon, the visa for Nepal began to smoulder like a burn pit. 'Hey loser, you still have to finish your trip around the world! Do you want to come home like a cormorant with drooping wings?'

This thought coiled around me like a snake, whispering to my ear, 'Stop with that so-called kingdom, get out of here. Show some guts and use that visa for Nepal. Hit the road again for Australia. That kingdom can wait!'

The Voice said, 'Seek first My Kingdom, and I will give you everything.'

Then the forked tongue hissed, 'You've found your eureka—fine. Be happy and get moving. Get out on the highway, looking for adventure. You were born to be wild, remember?

On one of my walks in the hills, I met an attractive woman in her thirties with raven-black hair and a long black dress. She was sitting in front of a stone cottage, and the accent immediately betrayed her being Dutch. It was the first I'd heard Dutch in months.

She was waiting for her Indian boyfriend, who hadn't shown up. I enthusiastically told her about my eureka moment since arriving at Hamilton House.

A few days later, she came to see me and asked, 'When will I see you again soon, Maurits? I'll wait for you with chai.'

Peter saw the lady and warned me, 'Morris, you'd better not visit that lady. She might seduce you, Satan is always smarter than you think.'

Would the devil have disguised himself as a black-dressed lady, as Peter suggested? Indeed, that temptation lurked like a cobra. I was longing to move to her and even to her cottage. I had already taken into account the possible confrontations with her Indian boyfriend.

The voice whispered, 'Why don't you ask this woman to travel to Australia with you? She must have some money or connections and remember, that kingdom will come later—it can surely wait.'

Hypocritically, I challenged the Lord, asking if He could point out the right woman to me, as I had just read the story of Rebecca and Isaac.

Behold, the next day, there was a five-page letter from Esther in Gouda. What a coincidence! She wrote that she had been waiting for me for almost a year. I was flabbergasted and happy. I hesitated, weren't the encounters at the Reeuwijkse Plassen just fleeting summer calf love? She was barely sixteen and like me, the black sheep at home. Literally—she was the only one of the three daughters who was not blonde, yet still fair-skinned. We had hours of in-depth conversations in the little sailing boat on the lakes. She was also searching and I enthusiastically began writing her letters full of Bible verses.

Walking along the mountain paths, with ferns and moss-covered trees, I wrestled further with life's most important question, while the woman in black lured me like a mighty magnet.

'Lord, for most of my life, I've always gotten the short end of the stick. Now I want to come out on top and for the long term. I want to give you a chance to prove that you and your Word are true.'

I had nothing to lose, only to gain, I thought.

'Take the Dutch lady to Nepal,' the voice of the black viper shrilled.

'If the Almighty promises to give me everything, including an arrival in Australia and absolutely everything, then I would be super stupid to ignore that offer.'

'Do you believe these promises? It's nonsense, man!'

'Yes, I'll go for the all-inclusive deal.'

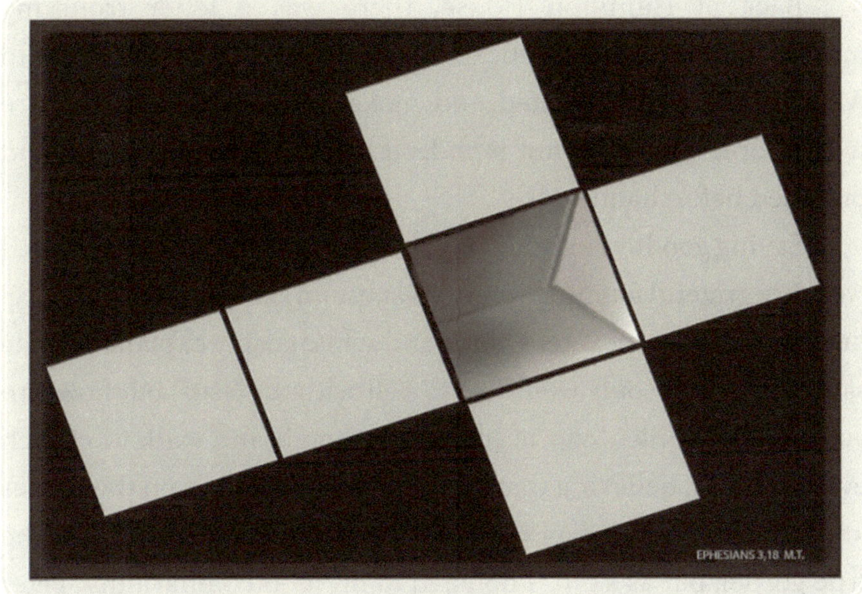

Ephesians 3.18

At the age of 21, I made the most important decision, I was going to risk my life with God. Was it a real risk? He had already helped me this far and saved my life in Rishikesh, so why not trust Him for the rest of my life?

'Okay, Lord, let's make the deal.'

Like Abram, who had been called from Ur in Iraq to the promised land, I made a kind of covenant.

'Lord, I will turn around and seek Your kingdom. In return, You promise to give me everything, which includes my arrival in Australia.'

Back at Hamilton House, there was a letter from my mother with an Air India ticket for July 21st—a one-way flight to Amsterdam! Flabbergasted and moved, I stammered, 'You are witty, Lord. The covenant is indeed mutual—you arranged and provided beforehand.'

Saying goodbye to Peter and Dorothy gave me mixed feelings. I was very grateful for my seven-week stay and the eureka experience, but I couldn't accept Peter's black-and-white gospel explanation. He said millions of souls would go to hell without Jesus, but how can you quietly drink a cup of tea on the porch and walk to church every Sunday, believing that all those poor wretches on the planes are lost? To Peter, I may have already seemed apostate from the true gospel, but as a gift, I donated to my 'good Samaritans', Peter and Dot, the money that was transferred to Stan's bank account via the check.

From Dehradun, I took the train to New Delhi and flew to the Netherlands on 21 July. Back then, you still got real cutlery on the plane, and I hereby confess that I 'borrowed' a spoon from Air India as a souvenir.

STAGE 9

Doorn

Dressed in 'Indian pyjamas', I arrived at Schiphol Airport and looked around in amazement at the enormous wealth. My happy relatives, dressed in the latest fashion, fetched me with a car without dents. We whizzed along the black asphalt highway with white stripes and fat, black and white cows grazing in green meadows. At home, the backyard was in full bloom with fragrant roses. In the living, we sat on thick leather sofas set on deep-pile carpet.

Stumbling between English and Dutch, I talked enthusiastically about my eureka moment. Mother had expected a cult member and sought a counsellor. In the phone book, she simply searched under 'Christian' and at the 'Christian Secondary School,' which I once attended, someone from the administration was a Christian, Mr. Vellekoop. He and his wife were present when I arrived home. Later, this couple invited me once a week to chat over freshly ground coffee and homemade buttered ginger cake. Invariably, the meetings always ended with prayer, after which the room glowed in a warm, holy haze. I liked Alice, who, despite her advanced age, was still witty, artistic and unruly. In addition to sculptures and paintings, she had created a stained-glass mosaic on her front door. On Sundays, these saints took me to a Baptist church in Alphen, where I had to get used to the straight, happy-clappy people.

After a few weeks, an evangelistic weekend was scheduled and since this hippie from India had 'seen the light,' I was expected to give a testimony on the street. The leadership was in the hands of a sympathetic young evangelist couple from New Zealand, whom I saw as a glimpse of God and part of the deal.

Friday evening was spent preparing for the coming Saturday, and while sitting in a large circle around the couple, I asked my most pressing question: 'How can a God of love send His creatures to damnation?'

The evangelist couple was silent for a moment.

'This is an important question that Morris is asking now. He spoke of a God of love—will He send people to hell?'

Silence again.

'Is God love? Is everyone convinced of that?'

Everyone nodded, except me.

'God proves it every day by raising the sun since time began. It is a star, giving just enough light and warmth on Earth to make everything grow. The Creator Himself is greater than the sun, and His love and grace are always more abundant than we can ever realise. I now think of Jesus' words after they crucified Him. Father, forgive them, for they know not what they do. Who would do that?'

He specifically looked at me.

I nodded, and he asked, 'Can love exist without justice? A loving father should also be righteous, right?'

I remember my father as very loving, but he could also become quite angry when I misbehaved.

'If God is love, light, and warmth, He can never and will never force people to love Him or choose His light; otherwise, it is not real love, correct?

The choice to enjoy His love and warmth is ours, here and now. He wants everyone to go to heaven and before you are worried about the whole world, be concerned about yourself first. When you get on a plane, the flight attendant will always ask you to take care of yourself first with the oxygen mask. After that, you can assist others. We first have to know Him personally, and then enlighten others. Are you satisfied with this answer?'

Silence.

I responded, 'So you have to accept that black-and-white gospel. It's all or nothing, just like in the desert when you're offered water or like a drowning person at sea who is thrown a lifebuoy. Take it or leave it?'

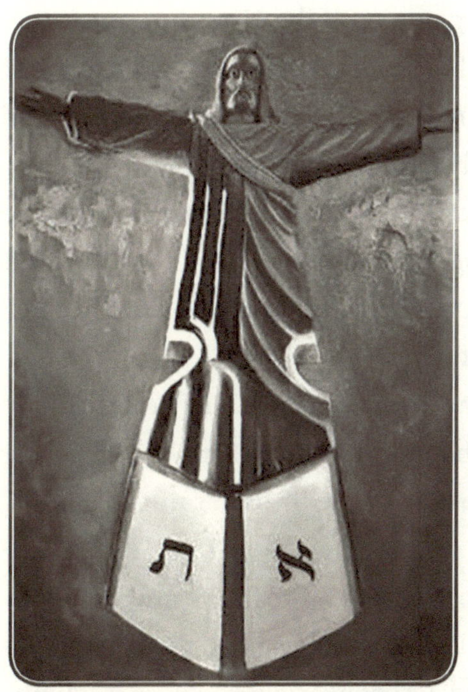

Aleph/Taf

Then the woman answered, 'No, Morris. Remember that God is pure love and He will always say, take it! He will never say, leave it. That quote comes more from the enemy.'

Back in Gouda, it seemed as if a heavy wood clamp was tightened around my head. I wrestled with the paradoxical questions surrounding God's goodness and justice. The text, 'He who has the Son has life; he who does not have the Son does not have life', was grinding in my head and hung like a millstone around my neck. 'No one comes to the Father except through the Son', weighed like lead.

'Is there only one way?'

The chess game with the Grandmaster was ending without a draw. At dawn, I descended the stairs to the living room, completely exhausted. I knelt by the fireplace and 'pushed over my king piece'—I was checkmated.

How would I ever understand the Grandmaster, the Almighty, the All-Knowing? I surrendered. As if they were welding in heaven, a sacred star, soft and pure, dropped onto my head and engulfed me in holy light.

My ego had been crushed. Henceforth, I would be limping in the eyes of the world, but in Him, I had been given eternal life! Welcome to the club of the blessed saints! I couldn't sleep for three nights.

In the following days, I read the ancient Bible books as if they were personal letters addressed to me. I wanted to shout it from the rooftops and accost everyone, 'There is a living God who loves you too!'

People stared at me strangely or politely called me crazy.

Sister Jolanthe and Esther were the first to accept the foolish gospel and choose the Way.

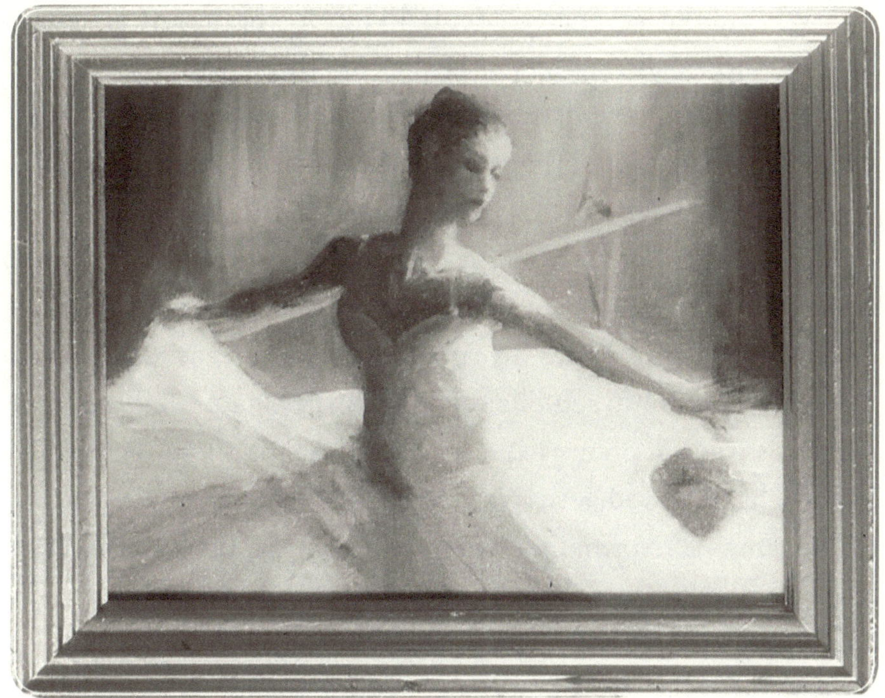

Jolanthe dancing for the Lord

Mother said she did not have to choose because she had been baptised as a child and had made her profession there. Two years later, she realised she could not inherit the Kingdom without being reborn.

I wanted to know everything about the Bible and Mr. Vellekoop pointed out the existence of an Evangelical Bible School in Doorn.

I still remember the beautiful ride in the late summer of 1973 over the sloping avenues full of autumn colours, like a heavenly road to the beautiful Schoonoord Estate. An enthusiastic Board of Directors welcomed me warmly and immediately admitted me to the study group.

With about seventy students living in the mansion, Joost, my down-to-earth roommate, helped me through the process of settling in. As a newborn believer, I was given Biblical 'meat' to digest. The walks with other students around the estate during the breaks were a relief.

Every evening after coffee, a student had to lead the day's closure and for my first turn, I was tense. Addressing such a large and advanced crowd with my first speech was no easy feat. I read the story of the miraculous feeding at the Sea of Galilee. The emphasis was not on my experience in Israel or the miracle itself, but on what followed. Jesus gave the surprising command to collect all the remains. 'Normally,' the scraps are left for the birds, but His disciples filled no less than twelve baskets with leftovers.

In my little sermon, I mentioned that at Bible school, bags of stale bread and pans full of potatoes were fed to the ducks daily. In India, I had seen hunger and felt it firsthand. Food waste should be out of the question. Why not fry the potatoes and how delicious is toasted bread?

The next morning, after breakfast, students brought baskets full of bread scraps to the table where I was sitting and said scornfully, 'Brother Tompot, you advised us to collect the leftovers, didn't you?'

The message had come through loud and clear, but when they arrived the next morning again with baskets, I became sad because I had high regard for these students and for the Word they were ridiculing.

Whether there is a causal connection with the next event in the dining hall, I don't know. It happened just before lunch, which had just been prepared for 70 students and some staff members. We had to wait for the bell before everyone was allowed to enter the dining room.

A few minutes before the ringing, half the stucco ceiling came crashing down with a thunderous roar. Frightened, we came to look and saw through the dust clouds, that huge pieces of debris had fallen right through tables and chairs. Apart from the many wounded, students would certainly have been killed. Thank God there was no one in the dining room at that time.

A new lunch was energetically prepared in the sitting room, and later, the ceiling was repaired with soft board, and no one talked about it anymore. This event made an overwhelming impression on me, and I asked an older student during a walk in the woods, 'Jacob, why did God allow this?'

'Ah, that's the classic 'why' question. Why is there so much misery in this world? Why are children sick or dying? Why are earthquakes and tornadoes killing innocent people? Why did my husband become depressed and commit suicide? The well-known questions blame God for everything. Can the Almighty prevent all the misery? Sure, He can!'

Sarcastically, I added, 'No wonder so many people drop out of the faith because of the misery in the world or the close circle of family or friends.'

'Maurits, let's try and ask how it could have been prevented. Was it overdue maintenance? Was the fault with us? If you think about it carefully, ninety per cent of all misery in the world is on our account. A different mindset is to ask why we have been saved from this great calamity and not to hold a thanksgiving service.'

'Did you know that God accuses us as well?'

I was surprised, and Jacob continued, 'I was naked, but you did not clothe Me. I was hungry and thirsty, but you didn't feed Me or give Me something to drink. I was in prison, but you didn't visit Me.'

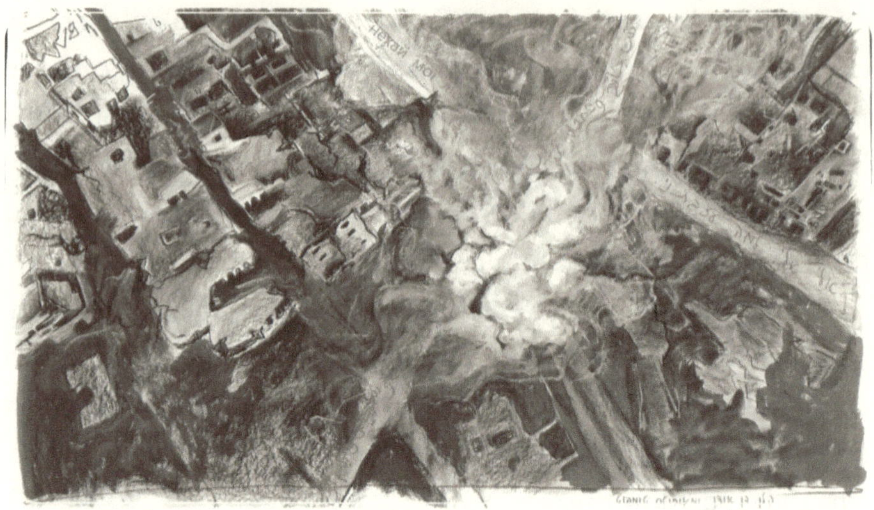

Dresden, Aleppo, Gaza
In two crossing streets of Aleppo or Gaza letters in Hebrew and Arabic,
'Why have you forsaken me? --- 'I was naked, but you did not clothe Me.
I was hungry and thirsty, but you didn't feed Me or give Me something to
drink. I was in prison, but you didn't visit Me.

I thought to be smarter than Jacob and asked, 'Could He not
have prevented all the misery from the beginning?'

'You mean with Adam and Eve? Sure. In that case, He had to
create Adam and Eve as robots or handsome monkeys.'

'Okay, but why didn't He make us resist the temptation?'

'Would you like a well-behaved or the smartest robot as a
child? Do you ever play chess against yourself, Maurits? You have
to do that at some point; it's not exciting, but quite boring.'

I didn't know how to answer.

'It's one or the other, a robot or a being with free will; nothing
as a creature in between. It's either a man, woman or animal; please

realise how unique we are with our free will. The other side of the coin is that we can turn against the Creator, and since the fall of man, this has happened on a large scale.'

Like the devil's advocate, I played my last trump card, 'Yes, Jacob, we'll soon be perfect robots in heaven, won't we?'

'Ah, you will certainly be the best saint in the first row!' Jacob laughed heartily.

'Why lose our free will in that timeless, holiday true paradise, called heaven? Why turn your back on God? Hold on, you have a point, Maurits, once upon a time, there was a rebellion in heaven by an archangel, Lucifer. This 'Light-bearer' was banished from heaven with a group of fallen angels, and they landed on this planet. This is probably why the earth became desolate and empty as written in the second sentence of Scripture. A re-creation or restart took place, which took six days. Peanuts for the Almighty,' Jacob laughed again.

At this 'prophets school', I rolled from one revelation to the next. One-third of the Bible turned out to be prophetic, and the book of Revelation is the capstone of all previous prophecies. Without knowledge of earlier prophets, the Apocalypse is an incomprehensible book, unfortunately still for many theologians. The Bible is the eternal bestseller, composed by one Author, incomparably inspiring like no other book in the world.

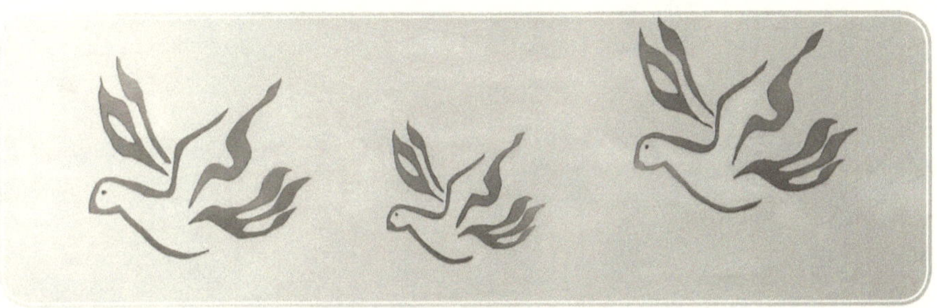

Triple shalom

STAGE 10

Norway

In the Gospels, I read, that he who comes to faith, will be baptised and in Gouda was no church where to be baptised. The only church in the immediate vicinity was 20 miles away, the Baptist church in Alphen, where I had already attended services with the Vellekoops. As Jesus showed the example by allowing Himself to be completely submerged in water by John the Baptist as a symbol of His death and resurrection, I obeyed His request and later Jolanthe and Esther followed.

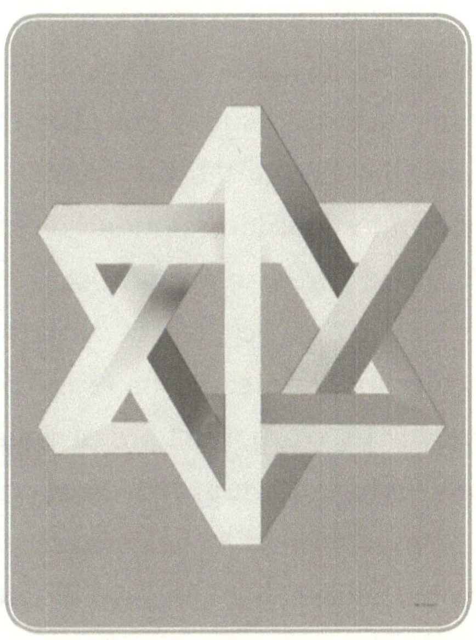

Eureka II

We found a spiritual home in a small evangelical church in Spieringstraat in Gouda, although the churchgoers had aged. With the start of a children's club, the congregation slowly blossomed like a mustard seed, and soon, I was even allowed to preach on Sundays.

Close by was a public school that young Ruud attended, and I was asked to teach Bible lessons to the fifth and sixth grades as a workplace student. In the meantime, Esther also commenced studying in Doorn, where I graduated after three years. My mother was proud since I had the status of a second-degree religion teacher.

Soon I got a job as a religion teacher in Overschie and later in Boskoop. The prodigal son had finally landed on his feet.

I could temporarily rent an apartment on Turfsingel, a sunny place along a canal and I was happy. After a few months, the tenant suddenly appeared from abroad earlier than expected due to a car accident.

One of the church members showed me an apartment above the church building that had been empty for years. It was neatly whitewashed, wallpapered and carpeted as preparation for the arrival of the Director of the old men's home. The purpose of the huge building had changed and I was allowed to live in the beautiful apartment as an 'anti-squat' guard on the south side. On the north side of the 'Vroesenhuis' lived a couple, I had never seen before. For only a hundred guilders a month, including gas, water and electricity, I rented three spacious rooms in that sixteenth-century building in the city centre of Gouda. It was on one condition, the accommodation could be terminated within three months. According to His Word, the Lord provided. I enjoyed this romantic spot overlooking an overgrown courtyard with a giant fir tree, where a few magpies nested. What a happy prospect that after Esther had completed Bible school, we would settle here until our long-awaited calling for Israel was activated.

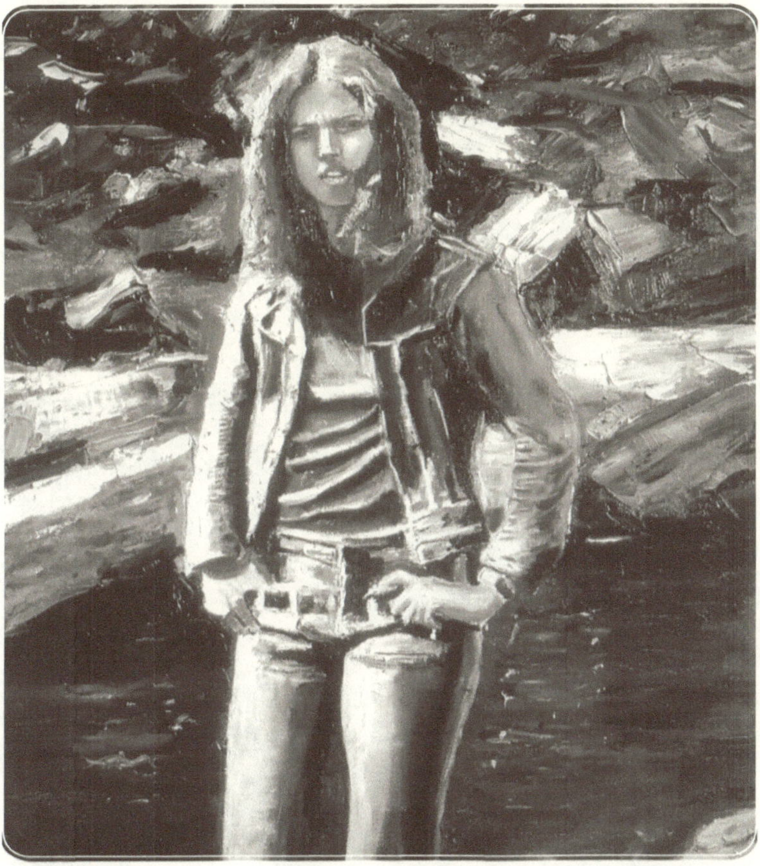

Norway hike

In June 1974, Esther's parents invited me for an unforgettable holiday in Norway. Walking into the wild between the fjords was like a hike in the Garden of Eden. We were engaged and everything looked bright and happy. Did we conquer paradise? Was the snake dead?

To be continued in the next stages of Route 777

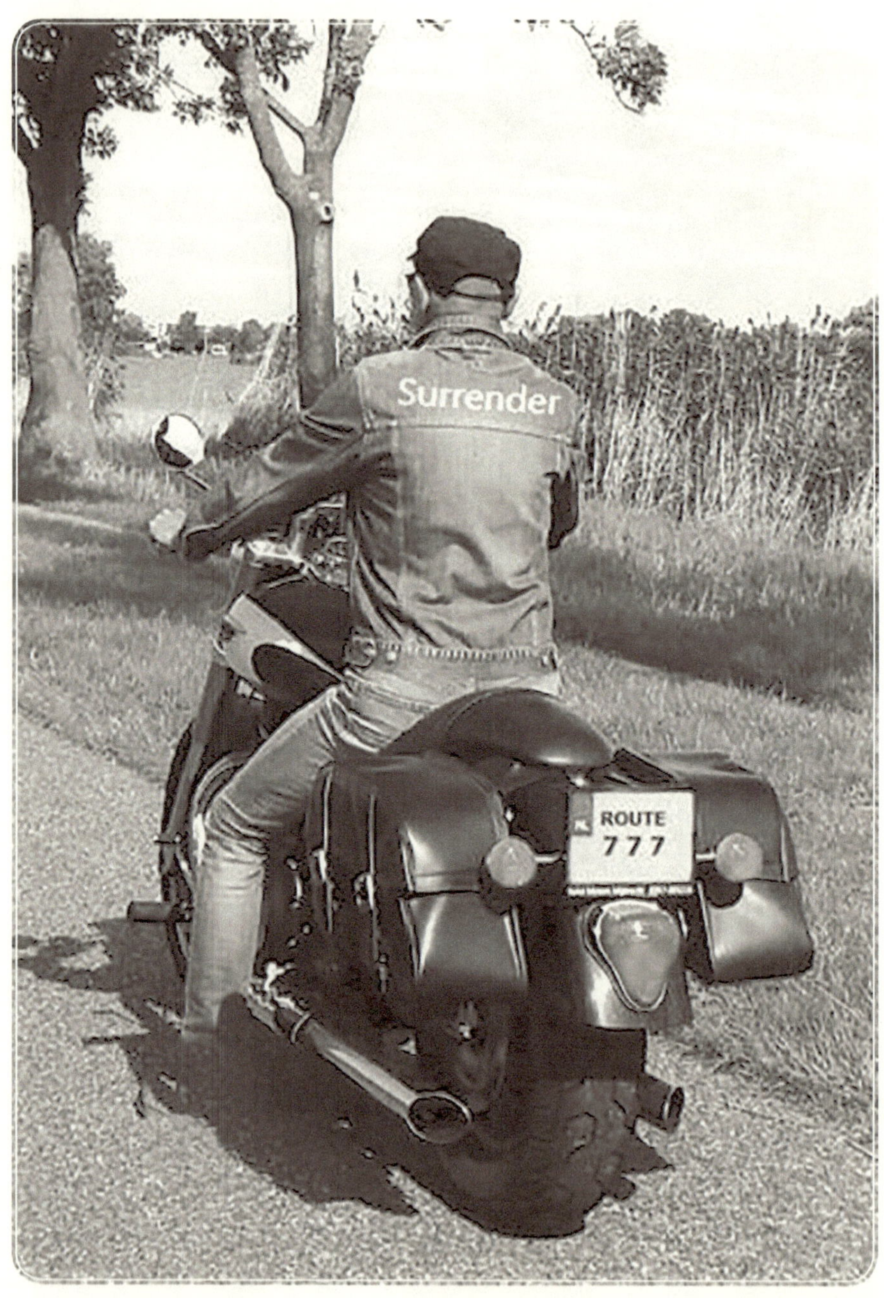

Surrender
ROUTE
777